THE L

AND OTHER STORIES

BY

SILVANO BISTAZZONI

DEDICATION

To my parents, partner and kids, for their love
and support

TABLE OF CONTENTS

The Locked Self and Other Stories

CHAPTER 1

"Hello, welcome to the therapy room, how are you?" I said.

He didn't answer, looking at me with his big dark eyes. He looked away as if he was looking for something to do.

"Would you like to play? There are many toys under the shelves over there," I continued.

He looked in the direction I was pointing and quickly walked towards the shelves, pulled the first big box of toys out and picked a toy car and before I could say anything, he threw it towards the window.

He missed it by a couple of inches; the car hit the wall and crashed onto the floor with soft tin clamor - completely smashed.

"That's a nice start," I thought. I didn't even have the time to tell him the therapy rules. "I'll do it now," I thought, getting closer to him.

"Jo, this is your time with me, you can do whatever you like here, but, there are a few simple rules which I think it will be nice you know: you can't break anything in the room, you can't hurt anybody including yourself. Is that clear?" I said.

He looked at me inquisitively and then replied.

"What happens if I do?" He challenged me.

"Guess," I replied assertively. I knew he wouldn't answer. I was now ready to formulate the regular contract.

"There's more before we start. Everything you tell me here is confidential, that means that I will not say anything about what you tell me to anybody, family, schools, friends. But, if I understand that someone is hurting you or you could hurt someone, including yourself, then I will have to tell people about it, but I will inform you first if possible."

"Is it clear?"

"Yeah, yeah..." he went on mocking me, "I didn't want to come here," he said.

"You didn't want to come here, but now that you are here, we can use our hour by doing stuff together," I replied.

"I want to go back home," he continued smacking a plastic dinosaur on the floor.

"I am sure your mum will come on time to pick you up as soon as we finish our time together here in the clinic."

He became silent.

I could see he was thinking about it, then:

"How many kids do come here?" He asked.

"Many kids," I replied, "at least five or six every day."

"And what do you do with them?"

"It's more like what they do with me," I answered. "We play, talk, read, write with the computer, paint, draw, whatever they'd like to do, and is ethical."

"What's behind that door?" He asked.

"Would you like to know what's behind the door?" I repeated.

Silence from him.

"There is another therapy room for older children who prefer to talk rather than play. Would you like to see it?"

He didn't answer, but I knew he would ask me again once he started to trust me.

"Ok, we have about 30 minutes together now, how would you like to spend them? We could play, what about that?"

"I don't want to play," he said.

"Ok, you don't feel like playing. What about drawing? You can start with this: draw a house and a person. I will start mine." He was sulking.

"Look there; there's drawing paper, paint, crayons, finger paints. If you need any help ask me, ok?"

He didn't reply. "I see you feel like you don't want to answer my questions, fine by me. I am busy doing my drawing anyway," I repeated, sitting on the floor with him, "if you need any help just ask, alright Jo?" He gave me no answer. "While I'm drawing and coloring would you like to tell me what sort of week have you had?"

Time together went on the same way, Jo says nothing or looks numb, while I ask questions now and then and observe with no response from him.

"Ok, we only have a few minutes left, is there anything you want to ask me?" A sharp sound of a bell broke the silence. I just realized that time was up.

"This is the bell telling us that they've come to collect you, Jo."

He stood up from his zombie-like state and started to walk towards the door.

"See you next week. I trust you can find reception on your own," walked out of the door.

. checked that he was going in the right direction. I could see his mother and the receptionist smiling, waiting for him.

Not a word was said, and together they walked out into the cold December evening. Looking out of my window I saw two fragile silhouettes walking in the street.

The session gave me a good opportunity to observe my patient and make the first assessment of the case.

Anger, of course, was very evident, as were depression and apathy, all related to neglect at an early stage.

His referral notes gave me some insight into his upbringing. It was easy to understand that his mother was a victim of the same treatment.

There has been violence in the family and abuse, Jo suffered from lack of paternal guidance and a paternal role model to follow.

The mother evidently cares about the children, but is she able to give them enough love?

Difficult to say, given the size of the family, with three children to look after, all very young, with no help from her partner or family. Neglect and attachment issues were most certainly a cause, even if she does love the children very much and tries to keep them safe with her.

Would the children get better care away from the mother? Probably yes, if they were lucky. However, there were other things to be taken into consideration, many things. The newspapers and television are full of news of abuse and neglect towards children. It is difficult to answer that question.

I tried to imagine their life.

What happened after the therapy session? Who was looking after the other children as they were waiting for them to get home?

Was her partner still living with them? And how do they respond to a new man in the house?

I know children can get used to anything if it means being able to live with the parents they love.

However, were they looked after properly or was the mother just thinking about herself and her sexual gratifications?

I always ask myself, what makes the children have the courage to disclose physical or emotional abuse during therapy. To confess it is difficult for a child, because most of the time they wrongly accuse themselves of causing it. When in a family with a single parent there are three children to look after, all from a different father, one begins to wonder if, in this type of family setting, they can enjoy a proper and ethical upbringing.

There is, of course, foster parenting and children's care homes, which are not always successful, for the child who in most cases would prefer to live with the biological parents.

Of course, there have been successful outcomes in many cases of fostering, also in cases of single parents finding the right person to fit and love the acquired family. Someone that will look after them. In most cases, the new arrival resents the fact that there is more than one child in the family and feels responsible for looking after them. Not surprisingly, after the passion has worn out, he disappears leaving the partner and children in a bad way, much worse than he had found them.

Mainly, it's all based on the fact of the children being lucky to get a step-dad who doesn't drink, is not physically abusive and doesn't interfere with them in other ways.

"Where the hell have you been?"

"I told you, it was Jo's first therapy session. We have just come back."

"This therapy session lasted four hours!"

"I had to collect him from the school, then take the train, wait an hour, and here we are,"

"It's 5 o'clock! These brats are driving me crazy."

"We stopped at the station for a coffee; Jo wanted ice cream... It couldn't have been so bad."

"No? It was bloody worse. Don't do it again, I have places to go.'

"Couldn't you have prepared something to eat for the kids?"

"It is your bloody responsibility. Don't do it again. Understood?"

"Fine, fine ... Don't worry. It is not that you don't live here, is it?"

"What the hell do you mean, you silly woman?"

"Well, I mean, if you live with us you have to accept your responsibilities as well as to share the advantages."

"Advantages? I don't see any advantages!" He shouted.

"Look, it has been a long day. I am tired now, and I have to prepare food for the kids."

"Don't mind me; I am going to the pub."

"That's it! 'I'm going to the pub,' she mocked him, "you are going to the pub every bloody evening and come back drunk. You wake the kids."

"Shut up," he replied, "enough of your chatter, I am going." The door slammed shut.

Allison looks at the kitchen: it is a mess. The children were trying to cook some food. To make a cake possibly.

There was flour all over the place, eggs on the floor and sugar everywhere.

The little one came in and started crying while Mary was sulking in a corner.

"What happened to you, Mary?"

"It was him," she said pointing at the door. "He was shouting at us. He was pulling little James by his arm, and when I tried to stop him, he slapped me."

"Ok, I am here now, and he's gone."

"He'll come back drunk, as you said, and start fighting with you."

"Let's prepare something to eat alright? What about a pizza? There are two salami ones to share in the fridge. Mary, go and get them, I'll set the oven ready," Mary looked at her mother helpless but walked towards the fridge to get the pizzas as her mother asked her to do.

The second session came, and I was determined to start a rapport with little Jo this time. Lots of things and hypotheses were going through my mind. How was he going to respond to my attempts to start a working relationship with him? Did he have enough time to think about last week's session? Will I notice any change in his behavior?

How did the family respond to the fact that Jo was having therapy?

Was his mother still happy about the fact that Jo had to come to the clinic every week, maybe for a long time? Sometimes, sessions end with logistical problems as well as psychological ones.

Distance to travel, expenses, frustration when improvement is not achieved immediately, jealousy, fear from the parents or caregivers, thinking that the child could say something about them which would jeopardize their arrangement or even take the child away from them, as in the case of a child who discloses harm or abuse.

Many things are to be taken into consideration. Those were my thoughts; just before little Jo came through the door, looking exactly as he did the last time. Time can be a healer, but can also make things worse. I was hoping that it wouldn't be the case with Jo. In any case, I was ready and willing to work with him. Experience taught me to be patient and to go slowly with the child, rather than trying to force rapport. Respect, silence, and empathy are also other very important things which have to be taken into consideration. In front of me there was a child who for nine years had some love from his mother and a lot of neglect and carelessness too. He was a special human being and needed respect and honesty to start a working relationship with him.

CHAPTER 2

"Hello young man," I said. "Come in, please. Can you pass me those books on the desk, please?"

Jo didn't respond. He looked as miserable as in the first session.

I thought a good activity for us to get to know each other, would be putting back the many books in the therapy room and dividing them.

Something quite easy to do, dividing the paperback book from the hardback ones. I chose this task because it was not difficult to do and quite easy to recognize the difference between the books.

"This is only going to take a few minutes, and you will be helping me a lot if you pass me those books please," I was surprised when he finally moved towards the books and was trying to spot the difference between them.

"Yes, Jo," I encouraged him. "These are hardback; they are a bit heavy, just pass them to me, one at a time."

"The others are lighter and smaller, easier to carry,"

He didn't look as if he was enjoying the task and I took no notice of his attitude.

Eventually, I started to help him with the movement of my body. A few signs helped my intentions because he started to walk towards the books.

The first one was a hardback psychology book, quite heavy, which he picked up from the table and started to walk towards me.

"Thanks, Jo," I kept saying. "I can see you are strong!" I said, grabbing the book and putting it on the shelves.

"That's it, hardback first three shelves, lighter ones above. Are you alright Jo?" I asked casually.

"You keep asking me if I am alright," He said with a grumpy expression.

"What would you rather like me to ask you?"

"Don't know!" The classic answer... but at least he was talking.

I kept silent for a few minutes. I try not to pressurize the kids in the therapy room.

They get enough pressure at home, at school, with the other kids, trying to comply with everything the adults ask them to do or to be.

In my case, some progress needs to be achieved. After a long silence, I asked:

"At what time did you get home last week, after seeing me?" I questioned him tentatively.

He was picking up three paperback books from the table. I gave him time to answer.

"It was five o'clock. We were late, mum said, and Bill had a go at us."

I understood Bill was Allison's latest partner.

"Five o'clock doesn't seem too late a time to arrive at home, does it?" I asked.

"That's what mum said, but he still shouted at us, and the kids were upset. They said he wanted to lock them up in the bedroom."

"What was the problem then?" I continued.

"What do you mean?" He asked to clarify the question.

"Is Bill always like that?"

"Yes. He's always having a go at us, especially when he is drunk. Last time he had a go at me because I didn't want to go to bed at seven. I bit his hand."

"What did Bill do when you bit his hand?"

"He grabbed me and started to shout at me."

"What did your mother do?"

"She was not there. She was with the neighbors asking them for milk. We ran out because Bill forgot to buy it."

"Does Bill get drunk often?"

"Yes, every night, he comes back home very late and wakes us up."

"What happens then?"

"He makes a lot of noise and starts breaking things."

"What does your mother say about it?"

"She tries to stop him, and then they have a fight, and it's difficult for us to go back to sleep."

"Has Bill ever hurt you in any way?"

"Mum always asks, but I am tired of answering the same questions."

"Nevertheless," I continued. "It is important to know; you are only nine years old. You have to be protected, and your brother and sister as well."

That reminded me of when I was about 12, something that happened in my school, in the toilets outside the playground area, next to the football pitch, where we used to play with all the residents of the college, older boys included.

I was in there, and two other boys were playing, splashing water at each other and giggling.

I was not part of it, only a curious casual observer. Somebody had noticed because I was called into the office by the headmaster.

He was a priest, with big round eyes and a big stomach. What they called the "consigliere" was there too. He was a much younger priest; we used to call him nasty. He was always looking for trouble and to punish us. Incredibly at that age, I knew already what it was all about.

They were afraid the boys were playing inappropriate games, and obviously, they were concerned about it, or was it just to alleviate their boredom? I played the naive boy, pretending I didn't know what they were getting at and I told them exactly what had happened.

They were splashing water over each other and nothing else. Obviously, they believed me because nothing happened after that. That's to demonstrate that children of an early age know a lot more than what we adults think they know.

It is obvious Jo knew exactly what I was going on about, and I was satisfied with his answer.

That didn't mean he couldn't have been abused earlier by other people or even by the same man, or woman.

There was also an issue of protection here, towards a man who was probably an alcoholic and didn't have any parental skills.

Can a man like that be a good parent? On the other hand, can you accept or believe everything a child tells you?

A child will resent anybody who will come between him and his mother, especially if he had a bad experience in the past and suffered neglect and loneliness.

The latest Social Service report will help me understand more about the dynamics of the family.

Our job as supporters is not to condemn or judge anybody or investigate, but safeguard the welfare of the child.

That is paramount, and nothing will alter the fact that the child needs to be protected.

The activity with the books went quite well. More than half an hour had gone by then, and there were only four books on the table to put aside.

"I'm afraid there is no more space on the shelves. Any ideas of what to do with them?" I asked.

"Don't know!" He answered going back to his apathy…. "I'll tell you what. We'll leave them there for the moment until we know what to do with them," I continued.

"We still have 20 minutes to go, Jo, how would you like us to use the time together?"

I pointed to the sand tray; there was also a big box of objects and symbols.

"Older boys and girls like to fiddle with them, rather than play with toys," I pointed at the box.

Given Jo's mental disposition, I thought that he might find it more interesting to mess about with them.

"Jo, I am going to show you my favorite object in this box, can I?" I asked.

No answer, but he was interested. I went on opening the box.

There was a massive quantity of things that would interest children who needed to convey a meaningful message.

I thought that it was a bit advanced for him, and I was going to change the media and technique when he dragged out of the box a lock with a combination wheel and a name forged on the center in big capital letters.

It was a big, heavy, silver lock, made of metal. He observed every single part of it, the front, the back, sides, angles; he even listened to it while he was turning it around, in case it clicked or made any noises at all.

I was really surprised and interested in his close examination of the black circle of numbers.

He started to fiddle with that, looking at it closely and waving it around.

Children usually play with the lock for about 15 or 20 minutes trying to open it and find the combination.

Invariably they get frustrated and ask me to tell them the numbers.

I always say I don't know the combination, and it is the truth, I don't remember it, which is why I don't use it any longer.

There is no point in lying to children because they can sense it immediately. The lock was almost 20 years old.

It belonged to my bike, and the only reason why it is in the symbol box is that I couldn't remember the combination numbers. It would be impossible to find one like that, I tried, believe me, but they don't exist anymore; and anyway, it is good that no one knew the combination, I thought, it will keep him interested and active.

There was a child whom I had seen a few years ago. She had serious issues with Attention Deficit Hyperactive Disorder or ADHD. That means that it didn't matter what you said to her, she would not listen or pay any attention. She also had a problem with people who she thought had authority over her, that meant almost everybody, teachers, minders, parents, Social Services people, the psychologist, etc.

To be in the therapy room with her was more than a torture, it was almost unbearable. She would jump from one activity to another, in a matter of seconds.

There was a point of desperation in me, and I was thinking of throwing the sponge and referring her, maybe to a female psychologist, in case she had a problem with the opposite sex.

One day, she noticed I had a musical instrument in the corner of the therapy room, and suddenly she came out of her defiant indifference.

Just to annoy me further, she asked me if she could have a go at it. I nearly dropped down from the sky and boredom with surprise, and said of course; amazingly relieved she finally found something to do. She started to knock down the notes with fury and singing.

She went on for the full session playing, bashing the keys. I was afraid she would break it, but I didn't care.

I was so pleased she had found something she enjoyed doing.

Even if the sound and words were indecipherable, it had a pleasant appeal and originality. The sound felt as though it was coming from some ancient archetypes.

I immediately realized she had a talent for music and singing.

Her background also came from deprivation and neglect. Her mother had been a drug addict trying to give up her habit. Unfortunately, she died of an overdose a few years before.

They lived in an environment of squalor. In her past, there had been issues of physical and psychological abuse.

The girl was twelve, and she could go home now and then for a week to be with her dad.

All she did was join her gang of friends and start roaming the streets and getting into trouble.

Her father did not care. She also had trouble with the police and was placed under supervision in a care home.

The same year, just before I saw her, the children were taken for a week's holiday in Scotland. She spent all week being sad on her own, always angry at the world, and complaining about everything and everybody, while the other kids were enjoying themselves.

I tried to teach her some notes, but she would not listen, or more correctly, she would not have the capacity to listen and concentrate on instructions.

After a few seconds, she carried on bashing the keyboard.

One session, before she came in, I didn't feel as if I wanted to listen to her music again. I turned the instrument off, with the intention of telling her that it was out of order.

As soon as she came, she went straight to the keyboard beaming with joy. I felt a bit rotten for taking away that instrument of pleasure, but I pretended I didn't know anything about it and told her that I would have it put right for the next session.

Of course, she did not believe me. She tried to play it in any way possible, but to no avail, she then tried to take the plug out looking at me with fury.

Then she said with anger in her voice.

"You are all the same, no wonder I don't trust you! You are all liars."

Just then, I realized that by doing that stupid thing, I fell straight into what she was trying to prove.

She finally succeeded in putting me on a par with everybody else, all the liars of this world.

I understood a lot about her after that, and even to this day, I am not proud of that little stratagem. However, I still feel there's a limit to disrespect. In that case, making an awful noise with the instrument was not acceptable. I was trying to find the best way not to upset her.

Needless to say, she continued bashing the keys in the same way for many more sessions but rules were established: the first 20 minutes of the session were dedicated to music, the second part of the session was for playing, talking or whatever she wanted to do that day.

Some very good progress was achieved through the musical instrument at school, learning, in relationship with the other pupils, with the teachers, and at home.

I received very positive feedback before she was transferred to a different school, away from where I lived because she had reached the age of sixteen.

I would like to think that she continued to play the instrument, and learn through music. Maybe somebody will teach her how to compose because she definitely had talents to be nourished and discovered. Furthermore, when she was playing, she was a different person. She was happy, confident and free.

When it was time to go, Jo was still fiddling with the lock. He didn't say too much during this period, but I had another opportunity to observe him at play.

He was a very determined little boy. His investigation was quite methodical and strategic. He tried to open the lock not only by turning the dial but also by hearing the clicks of the combination and putting the lock in different positions.

The movement of his hand around the dial varied. He tried to give a fast action, then a slow one, then a reverse one and so on.

CHAPTER 3

The week after, when I was working at the clinic, I received a call from the Social Services lady who was in charge of Jo's case.

She told me that Jo had been temporarily put into care, and could not come to therapy for the time being.

This is something that can happen when dealing with children. Every therapist dreads this moment because the sessions are put on hold, and you never know when you are going to see your patient again.

It is annoying when this happens, but there is nothing you can do, just be resigned to the idea.

I tried to imagine how Jo must have felt.

This is the main concern, and everybody should be aware of that: the feelings of the child.

From Jo's record, I understood very well that he did not like to stay with foster parents. In addition, from the information from the Social Services, it was easy to understand that he witnessed a fight between his mother and her partner.

How bad was it?

Was Jo hurt?

Will he be able to return to some kind of normal life after that, or will he be left in strange hands?

Difficult to say when the Social Services or the police get involved. On the other hand, is the parent capable of looking after three children?

I have dealt with many cases like this one, and I know they keep reoccurring until something very serious happens, and the children are taken away from their biological parents.

It is easy to predict what the future holds for a kid like Jo, who is used to neglect, rejection, and violence.

Some children get used to coping with anything if they can have some kind of real family life.

All this was going through my mind when I received another call from a man who I thought was Bill, Allison's partner, wanting to make an appointment to speak with me.

Would it be possible?

I must admit, I was puzzled by his request and the reason that had prompted him to ring me. The man sounded very concerned and sincere.

I made an appointment to see him the next day during my lunch break. Many issues were going around in my head after the call: the nature of the visit, whether confidentiality issues were involved here, further possible accusations, guilt, self - defense?

I decided that the best action on my part would be to listen to what he had to say and then come to my conclusion.

When Bill came, I was doing some work on my computer. I often do that, just before my lunch break, as I don't like to take notes during the session with my patients because it takes the focus away from them, and I want to dedicate my attention fully on them.

When I saw Bill, I was very surprised by his appearance. He wasn't at all as I had imagined: a man in his mid-forties, disheveled by alcohol and drugs.

In front of me, there was a handsome man in his late thirties, well dressed, well groomed and well spoken.

This is proof that sometimes you cannot trust your imagination, or assume too much about people, their appearance, personality, and attitudes.

After the introduction, I went straight to the point and asked him how I could help him.

It was evident that the visit was concerning Jo and the issues which led to the children being taken into care and the police caution against him.

At that moment, I wasn't aware of any court orders being produced against Bill.

His voice was well balanced, and his manner was polite and assertive.

I learned not to come to conclusions too quickly about people in cases involving children and young people.

Parents, foster parents, step-parents, and minders can transform themselves into Mr. Hyde if it suits them, but at the same time, I decided to give this man a chance.

"I am concerned with Jo and the other children. They don't like to be split up and sent to foster parents."

My first reaction would have been to answer:

"Perhaps you and your partner should have thought about that before all that happened," but I decided to stick to the program and encourage him to go on further.

"It was absolutely nothing, just an argument. It was that nosey neighbor. She has a thing about me."

"Bill, the problem is that when something like this happens, it is a concern of the police and the Social Services."

"I know, but, I wonder if you can do anything to help?"

"Like what?" I answered, looking at him.

"Like going back to normality. Jo was getting much better after seeing you."

"I appreciate your concern, but I think all I can do is to wait until they decide on the best program for Jo. I will keep myself informed about his welfare, but even that will be limited to the information they want to release. Allison will be able to get more information and possibly visit him."

"Ah, there's the problem, I don't know if I want to get in touch with Allison, not until things change. She is bombarding me with telephone calls, text messages wanting to see me, getting together again... I don't know."

"I hope a court order hasn't been issued against you or a police caution?" I asked him.

"No... They said it is a family dispute, we have to sort it out ourselves."

"That's not too bad then. So what has to happen for you and Allison to get back together again and avoid more problems with the kids?" I asked.

"A change of attitude on her part," he answered promptly.

I looked at him, puzzled, inviting him to explain further.

"Allison had a lot of problems with her ex-partners, and I mean problems. They were violent towards her and the children. Allison is very aware of this, but we are not all the same, are we? I really care about those children, even though their attitudes are very cold towards me, and I think it is Allison's fault instigating them to keep their distance from me. Most times, I feel like a stranger in that house. It is almost unbearable, and that is the reason that I drink. I don't have a problem with alcohol."

I could not resist interacting. "I appreciate what you said, Bill, but most people who have a problem with alcohol say that they don't have a problem with it," I replied.

"I know what you are saying, but it is the truth. I keep drinking to forget all the issues and problems of that family," he answered genuinely.

"What do you think is going to happen next?" I commented.

"I don't know! I wanted to talk to you and explain a little of what is going on. I am not the only one to blame," he answered.

"At the end of the day, the most important thing is the welfare of the children," I replied.

"I agree," he answered. "I don't know if getting together again would be best for the children."

"That is a decision that you both will have to make, as for the situation now, I don't even know if I am going to see Jo again," I replied.

"It frequently happens with children that have been taken care of by the social services." I added.

"I understand, you see, Jo is a very intelligent little boy. I thought we were getting on well together; there was a lot of communication between us and then suddenly ..."

"Anyway, I think the problem started a long time ago when Jo was three years old, and Allison got mixed up with a group of good-for-nothing friends in the area, particularly those mentioned before. Did Jo say anything about it?"

The man could have been very genuine, or maybe he asked not because he cared about the child but because he was trying to find something about himself, or he was just protecting himself from further actions. "I am sorry. I shouldn't have asked," he sighed.

The conversation was ending.

"I am sorry, but I have a patient who is due to come in five minutes' time," I said, rising from my chair.

The man responded by jumping up and saying. "Thank you for seeing me."

"That's fine!" I replied.

Children resent any lack of parental affection and guidance. I have experienced a lack of parental guidance myself.

My father used to work at sea and would only come home one or two days every month, if at all.

I used to envy all my friends who had a father at home; I used to cherish all the stories that they used to tell me about their fathers, even if that meant being punished.

I value so much even now the times that my father spent at home with us, my mother, two sisters, and elder brother.

My father was a good story-teller and had a very vivid imagination. He used to make up children's stories on the spot, and they were always original and inventive.

The ending was always a little macabre; for instance, the giant at the end would eat all the children, or the big wolf would terrify all the little ones before they went to bed, but somehow they didn't frighten us.

We'd be all together, in one bed with him who was protecting us, before my mother came to bed and we would be sent to our bedrooms.

It was a magical time, and I used to love it. I think that came from my grandmother. She was a kind, lovely lady, who had seven children and loved them all thoroughly.

I never heard my father talking about his family life, but somehow it was clear to me that he had a good, loving upbringing.

To this day, I regret the fact that we were not allowed to spend more time with our father, because of his job.

With my mother, it was a very different story. It is not that she didn't love us, far from it, but her personality was only allowing conditional love.

There was always something we had to do to deserve her love and affection, and sometimes it was hard going, especially for me, as I was the youngest child and I felt I had to fulfill that role.

She would say on a cold winter day, 'I am going to leave you forever. Nobody loves me here!' She would promptly leave the house and start walking towards the sea, which was not very far.

The frustration of living practically as a single parent and having to put up with two demanding girls, and my brother and me, sometimes got too much for her.

Inevitably, it was me, the one running after her saying, 'don't leave, please mum, don't!' Meanwhile my sister wouldn't move a finger, completely ignoring her, and my brother would probably be out chasing girls.

I really believed her. For me, she was going to leave us if I didn't stop her. To this day, I still wonder if I really managed to avoid the tragedy, several times, or if she was doing it for proof that we loved her.

I must say I was very surprised by the coldness of my sisters, but probably they were more intelligent than me. If she was looking to get some sympathy from them, I am afraid she didn't get any, ever.

I was very much a wanted baby. My mother had already had three children—two daughters, one son—and my parents desperately wanted another son for a reason I was never able to understand.

After my brother Tom, there was a miscarriage, and then I arrived, two years after, on a cold December night, Wednesday at two o'clock in the morning. According to my mother, when I was born, I was crying, and I never stopped crying for three nights, to the point that she asked my grandmother to throw me out of the window. That really upset my grandmother who from then on took care of me.

Apparently, she was always with me and cared for me until her death.

It is obvious that my mother didn't mean it. She told me years later, and funnily enough, it made me laugh. The thought of me, as a baby, flying out of the window and ending up in the sea somehow amused me.

My mother came from a farming background. My grandfather owned a farm not far from where we lived.

Her mother was a tiny little lady with piercing blue eyes, who had been looking after five children and helping on the farm all her life.

My grandfather, a very handsome tall gentleman, died relatively young and my grandmother and my mother took all the responsibility of the family on.

It was tough, looking after two young brothers and two sisters. The younger sister eloped with a farmhand when she was 15 years old. When my mother was 21 and tired of working on the farm, after the war, she became a nurse and worked in a sanatorium for tuberculosis patients. She often told us that she saw so much misery and death that she decided to get married as soon as she found a suitable husband. She had to wait quite a bit because, by the time she got engaged to my father, she was 29 and my father 30 years old.

I admire her honesty because we often told her that she was quite old before she got married and she always replied that she had her experiences, which by then was something quite difficult to talk about. Furthermore, it wasn't easy to please her. Later in life, I understood how much she loved us and all the sacrifices she made to make sure we grew up healthy and educated. During her life, she helped a lot of people in town, and they still remember her, for her kindness and support.

My father's background was completely different. He came from a business family not far from where my mother lived, by the sea.

The family owned properties in town and an emporium, then the only facility for shopping in the area.

It was a small town. My grandfather owned horses and used to take passengers from where he lived to the main center, about six miles away.

The story goes that when my grandfather met my grandmother, they fell in love instantly. My grandmother, Sara, was only sixteen and my grandfather 19 years old.

Sara's father, a wealthy landowner of the area, opposed the match. There followed a long period of frustration and subterfuge. Eventually, the two eloped from my grandfather's house. One night my grandfather managed to get into Sara's house, and the rest is history, as we say. Sara's father was extremely upset about it and disowned the daughter forever. He would refuse to see them again or their children, but they lived happily together for many years, and they had seven children. One of them, of course, was my father, the youngest of the lot, a bit like myself. People in town say that a song was composed about her, but I never heard it, and I don't know even today if it was true.

Apparently, Sara was an incredibly good-looking young woman. Even my mother often said that she was very kind, generous and beautiful, with a wonderfully sweet character, noted by everyone who had the good fortune to meet her. Of course, I don't remember her, even though as I said, she used to look after me when I was very young. I think she died when I was 2 or 3 years old. There are a lot of photographs of her in the old family album, and the beauty and the sweetness of her smile stood out a mile.

My grandfather, in contrast, was a dark, strong man, with a troubled character, but very generous and honest. Sara must have seen an endearing side of him when they met. Several pictures are there as a testimony to the difference between the two, and yet something they had in common must have united them. The proof is that they were very much in love for all those years they lived together. My grandfather was dead when I was born, which is probably why my grandmother also died prematurely. They loved each other immensely.

Jo must be missing all of this. No wonder he is confused. He never had the comfort of knowing his grandparents or a father.

Allison was raised in foster homes and care homes for children. There is a natural biological and psychological formation that is imprinted in all of us even before we are born. When we are born, we begin to recognize and get familiar with it. Naturally, it's a process that will not happen if our search has no foundations or reality. In the case of Jo, not knowing even his father is causing problems deeper than confusion and frustration. It's like being left in a desert suffering loss of memory.

Jo was taken away about a month ago, and I received no news from the Social Services, his mother or his foster parents. I decided to give them a call and ask them what was going on with the case.

CHAPTER 4

The assistant who answered didn't know anything about Jo and his family. The lady I always spoke to concerning Jo was on leave for two weeks.

That didn't make me feel better or satisfied. A sense of frustration took over me, but I managed to keep calm and ask her to ring me back when she got to know something or anything about Jo.

Of course, I prepared myself for a long wait. One week, two weeks, maybe a month. I would ring her again before the end of the week.

I decided to give Allison, Jo's mother, a call. It is perfectly ethical to do so.

Jo is one of my patients. Therapy was cut suddenly outside our boundaries, and I have the right to ask if he is alright or not.

I picked up the phone, and at the other end of the line, Allison answered promptly.

She sounded tired and apologetic.

"I am sorry I can't help you. I keep ringing them, and I get the same answers. They don't allow me to see him or talk to him. I am very angry about everything; I was hoping you could help me. Could I come and talk to you?" She sounded genuine and upset.

"Yes of course," I replied. "When would you like to come?" I asked.

"The sooner, the better," she said. We fixed an appointment, and I was quite pleased with her response.

There was some good news from the Social Service worker. I finally could catch her in the office and ask about Jo.

He wanted to go back home and expressed a wish to see me again soon. Meanwhile, he was back to his old behavior, lashing out and breaking things.

The foster parents were near to breaking point. They had already committed, with the social care worker, to fostering other children, who were due to come to them in the next ten days. She was suggesting that Jo could come back towards the end of next week and I could see him then.

I replied that it was a bit short notice. I reminded her that she had plenty of time to arrange everything and "what would have happened if I didn't ring her?"

She said, "Believe it or not, I was just about to pick up the phone and inform you of everything."

As usual, the Social Services people think that they are the most important body to safeguard the welfare of the children and they behave accordingly.

Just to let her stew a bit, I said that I would try to accommodate Jo, if possible, in the next fortnight but that meant that I had to shift many of my patients to another time. Anyway, I would let her know about my decision later.

Of course, I intended to see Jo, even if that meant giving up my lunch break. I was also pleased by the news, and I would have something positive to tell Allison when she came to see me the following day.

Things don't move fast when you are dealing with children and young people.

There are a lot of things and people to take into consideration, particularly when the child is involved in a dispute, suspected neglect, abuse and so on.

Patience is the most important skill that the therapist learns in dealing with them. Patience with bureaucrats is not one of my strengths.

I get frustrated and sometimes angry with them because they are like robots and you cannot argue with their robotic attitude.

Many of my students have not acquired the skill of patience yet and suffer the consequence when training. You can ask them so many questions, but you can be sure you will get the same answer. I always say to them, "you've got to have the patience or choose another branch of therapy or another profession."

They smile, and they keep suffering.

Therefore, at least I had that good news to report to Allison, with reservations of course. Was she going to change her way of life?

Was she going to choose the right partner, finally? Was she going to grow up and look after her children properly?

It is not a good start to complain after everything has gone wrong.

I know that type of mother, unfortunately. They tend to choose the same type of partner repeatedly.

Of course, it is not my place to tell them or warn them, but at the end of the day, the children are suffering because of their attitude and choices.

I was hoping that would have been a good lesson for her, even though I didn't dislike Bill. It is very easy to blame somebody else for your drinking and your behavior, and carry on with the drinking and abusing everybody around.

I gather there were two versions of Allison: the mother and the woman. The woman who wanted sex, and the mother who wanted to protect her children.

I could sympathize with her point of view, but I think you must be very careful with your choices when you have a young family to support.

What kind of man would ever think of having a long-term relationship with such a woman? She had to choose: protect the child or disobey her impulses. Not an easy choice for her, I thought.

Allison already knew that Jo was about to come back home soon. The Social Services people rang her the day before and told her. How did she feel about it?

'Over the moon,' she responded, but when were they going to leave them in peace?

I reminded her that if the children were taken into care, it would be no fault of the authorities but hers and her partner's, and "How is the situation now with Bill?" I asked.

"Was it going to happen again? Next time the Social Services could ask for a court order and take the children away for good."

"Whose side are you on?" she asked me angrily.

"I am on Jo's side," I replied.

"I am not convinced," she said. "The entire establishment sticks together."

I was careful not to lose my temper. "I am not the establishment; I am a neutral professional. I am telling you this because I have dealt with many cases like this one. I know the ending if you are not careful and you want to keep your children. I feel I should warn you of the consequences, so you won't have reason to accuse anybody else."

She calmed down, and she said she was sorry for the outburst. "It's not easy to look after three children and try to have a life at the same time," she said.

"How is the situation with Bill? Do you know he is concerned about Jo and came to speak to me?"

"The situation is as it was," she replied sharply. "He kept in touch, but nothing has been decided yet. He has always promised to give up drinking, find a job, and look after the children but it never seems to happen. He's fine for two or three weeks, and then the drinking starts again."

"Did anything happen to Jo during his presence, in the house or indeed with anybody else?" I enquired tentatively.

"You mean with another of my men? I know what you are thinking," she replied.

"I am not here to judge" I reassured her promptly. "I am thinking of Jo's welfare."

After a long silence, Allison started to speak again. "I suspected my previous partner of abusing the children in some ways. He was a violent man, but I never had proof. I can't go accusing people, and the children always refused to answer my questions."

"You are saying you suspected something. On what do you base your suspicions?"

"Well, from the children's actions. They were afraid of him. That's when I began to wonder whether something was happening." she said. "Even if it was shouting at them, I didn't like it! After that, I never left them with anybody else. But that meant I couldn't work anymore."

"How long ago was that?" I asked.

"About three years ago. That was when Jo's behavior started to go from bad to worse."

"How did the children respond, when you were asking them all those questions?"

She thought for a moment, and then she answered. "Strangely, I suppose, silent and then, I thought it was like trying to protect somebody or something. They never answered properly, but if I went shopping or something, I made sure they came with me if he was at home," she said.

You need to have stronger proof than that to accuse somebody of abuse, I thought. Maybe the children did not like him for many reasons. Then again, her partner could have been on the defense and that could create a false impression for a parent who is already worried, mainly because she knows her own shortcomings.

We are not investigators or the police, we listen and help children to cope with whatever happens or upsets them, to make their life uncomfortable and to protect them in any way possible from the perpetrators, but it must come from the children, not from us. We cannot judge or accuse anybody without first listening to our little patients, and then come to our own conclusions.

She seemed to be calming down now, having understood that I was only looking after Jo's welfare, and intended to follow the course of the therapy to the end.

Knowing that Jo was coming back obviously made her happy and she was looking forward to the reunion. However, was she going to change her lifestyle?

Was she going to forego her sexual life for the sake of the children? Strong-minded women with right principles would. They would sacrifice anything for the sake of the children.

Having met Allison, I understood that she was not such a woman. She would go on loving her children, but that would not stop her from connecting with her usual choice of partners.

Actually, looking back and having met Bill, I hoped that he would come back and start to live with them again. At least he wouldn't harm the children, I thought.

The time came for Allison to go. I told her "she could come back to talk with me anytime she wished, and I hoped she would have a good reunion with Jo and the other children."

CHAPTER 5

When Jo came back to the therapy room, two weeks after the conversation with the Social worker, he did not utter a word. He went directly to the box, threw all the toys in a heap on the floor and started searching them.

"Hello Jo," I said. "Nice to see you back here. How are you?"

He didn't answer but continued to search in the midst of the toys.

Was he looking for the famous lock? "If you tell me what you are looking for, I might be able to help you." No answer and he kept looking into the toy box.

"I was wondering when you'd come back Jo; it has been a long time. A month plus? Two months perhaps?"

He did not answer my question, but he looked at me. I took it as a positive answer; he was obviously pleased to be back.

"So, Jo, what have you been doing all this time? We can talk while you are playing, or we can play while you are talking." I joked, not expecting an answer.

"Your books are still on the table," he said. "You haven't done anything all this time?"

"You are right," I answered. "I have been very lazy since you left. Well, now you are here, we can continue working together."

He stopped searching, looked straight back into my eyes and said, and "where were you when I needed you?"

I was very surprised by his challenge. For a moment, I didn't know how to answer. I paused to reflect on my next move. This could be make-or-break point.

"Well Jo, I was hoping you would come back sooner, but it didn't happen as you know. I am sorry if you had to endure all that, I wish I could have done something about it."

"Blah, blah, blah," he answered mocking me, "You are all the same, words, words, words."

I wasn't going to let him get away with his remark. "What would you have me do instead?"

He didn't answer, went on playing. I decided to let him do what he wanted. The therapy had been interrupted for quite a long time. Restoring trust in the relationship would take time and effort. The child felt let down again, and the result was evident to me. It was up to him to communicate when he was ready and if he wanted to. I could only assist him and interact when it was appropriate.

Now he was playing with the farm animals; he was putting them all in a long queue. The horse was at the head of the line followed by a cow, a sheep, a pig, a hen, another sheep, a dog and a very small pig at the end. "Your animals seem to all go in one direction."

"Yes, they do, towards the sea," He said.

"They are going to the sea. The horse is at the head of the queue," I interacted.

"The horse is guiding them," he explained seriously.

"Will they have a long way to go?" I continued.

"Don't know," he replied.

"Mom took us to the seaside last year, we went by coach," he said.

"I see, you went altogether by coach to the seaside," I replied.

He found an old bus toy bus in the box and dragged it out; then he positioned it next to the animals. "That's how we went," he confirmed.

"You all went together to the seaside, you, your sister, your brother, mom, and Bill?"

"No, he didn't come. Mom didn't tell him we were going," he said sharply.

"I see. Bill didn't know you were going," I paraphrased.

"He didn't know. He was upset when we came back; they started to fight."

"Your mum didn't tell Bill you were going, and when you got back, Bill was upset about it and, started to fight with your mom?"

"Yes, that's what happened. The horse has been naughty now, look," he said, showing me the horse that was galloping away from the group.

"The horse is trying to get away," I said. "I wonder why?" I asked.

"That's what happens every time. I will stop it from getting away. Look!" he said, fastening the horse's legs with a piece of string he found in the box.

"I see." I acknowledged his action. "The horse can't get away now, and his legs are tight and secure. I wonder how the horse is feeling know."

The rest of the group was now all over the floor; the perfect queue had been upset by the horse's behavior.

There was no order or direction anymore. I pointed that out to him, and he didn't answer.

He just looked at the disarranged group and stood up as if he wanted to go.

"Can I go to the toilet?" he whimpered.

"Sure," I replied. "You know where it is and, when you come back it will be time to go."

Jo went to the toilet, and I started to put the animals in a circle to form a happy picture for when he came back.

When he returned, I was pretending to play with the family.

"Look!" I said, "They are very happy together, aren't they?"

He didn't answer and stood there looking at the animals.

"Jo, what do you think has to happen to make the family so happy?"

He didn't answer and, with a quick gesture of his hands and arms, destroyed the happy circle and started to walk toward the reception room, where his mother was waiting for him.

I was left there to ponder and reflect on the content of the session. Was Jo improving in any way? Was I confident enough to be able to challenge him and get a result?

Working with children is significantly harder than working with adults because progress is slower; there's nothing to help you to find out the clinical status of the child.

It takes you back to your childhood with all the passion, pains and experiences of the early years.

After that session, I couldn't stop myself from going back forty years or more to when I was Jo's age.

It was a trip to the country, the farm where my mother was born and became part owner of the property.

When we arrived, late afternoon on a hot summer day, we were tired and hungry.

The people who lived on the farm were distant relatives of my grandfather and his family, a mother and a son. I don't remember seeing her husband. The woman was tall and slim, about forty years old, with dark eyes and black hair. She was nice enough, but she definitely didn't go out of her way to make us feel at home, and we were the legitimate owners of the house. On reflection, I think now that all things had been studied and prepared by them to go in their favor. I didn't feel very comfortable in that house and I wanted to go back straight away.

My cousin, their son, was a thin boy with very pale skin and ginger hair.

He was very shy and didn't utter a word. My aunt, who lived abroad, was there too. Was the visit supposed to be a meeting to discuss the sale of the farm?

My mother didn't say anything, but that would explain the visit.

If this was the reason, why wasn't the head of the family there to discuss it with them?

My aunt was always very polite and kind, but she was as cold as an ice cube.

The single daughter of a local family, she married my uncle, my mother's brother, and they were very happy together. She was thin and pale, always smiling, but somehow that smile didn't mean anything. She was pleasant enough and always careful what she said even with the kids. It was evident that she was a very strong woman of character and in charge of the family.

They had two daughters, blonde girls with a sweet smile, very much like their mother while my uncle was a man of few words, a good-looking man but very passive and I think a bit reserved.

Strangely enough, my mother always had a soft spot for him.

She preferred him to the other brother who in my opinion was the most caring, kind man I have ever met in my life. Later, I used to challenge her by saying that her older brother, the one she preferred, never came to see her or tried to get in touch with her. On the other hand, the younger brother came to visit us every month to see how we were and if we needed anything, or if I wanted to go and stay with them for a month or two. She never explained the reason, and I didn't know what must have happened when they were young at home.

My mother's brother had a small family. He had one child, who when I was very young was like a brother to me.

That night we had to stay with them because it was too late to get back and they didn't even have time to discuss whatever they had to discuss. My cousin, who was shy and silent, became very talkative when we were sharing his bedroom.

I dreaded the morning, but it actually turned out better than I imagined it. I walked around the farm, and its beauty besotted me. It extended in fields and woods and there was even a stream running through it. The hot summer sun made it look quite magical. The house had potential, with several bedrooms, a lot of space and features. My grandfather must have been quite a man to afford such a property and the surrounding land, as I reckoned some years later. Not that my mother ever said anything about it, she could be quite stubborn if she didn't want to talk about something, and I was too young to be aware of what was going on. Children are not informed about all facts of life, as I understood later when I was able to gather bits of information from around the family. They don't consider that one day their children will be very much affected by their choices, decisions, and mistakes. Having said that, I must add that I loved, and still love, my parents, and I am glad they were not greedy or unjust towards anybody.

She never spoke about it again, and eventually we forgot about the land and farm. On reflection, I feel that following my father and giving up her job and her house must have felt to her like giving up her identity. Living in a new environment wasn't easy if you were an outsider in 1940. It took a long time for her to be accepted. She was considered a stranger in her own country. I know she suffered a lot.

That evening we left, having achieved and concluded nothing, I thought. There must have been a motive for us to go, and we departed silently.

There was an improvement in Jo's behavior, the boy was responding to my interactions. He was active during the sessions, and I knew he was looking forward to coming to see me. The time spent with the foster parents slowed the process down a little, but not as much as I had expected. There was also a change in his physical aspect. A boy of his age tends to grow quickly, even a month can make quite a difference, and he was getting stronger and more confident. His attitude towards his family members improved greatly; he had become more mature and understanding. I was looking forward to the next session, and I hoped it would be the same for him.

CHAPTER 6

The time for the next session came but no sound or sight of him. My secretary tried to ring his home, but no answer was received.

Something must have happened. Dealing with children is not a straightforward affair. If he was sick, someone would have told us, as usually happens. I hoped the Social Services wouldn't get involved again in what might be going on in the household.

I asked my secretary to ring the school which Jo attended and ask them if they knew anything about him and when was the last time they saw him.

The school was very cooperative as usual. The last time they saw Jo was three days before. They also had tried to get in touch with the mother, but they had no answer.

They had no news from the Social Services or the police, so they assumed that it was probably a family problem that was the cause.

It was a shame, the headmistress said, that it had happened when Jo was showing real improvement. His behavior had improved, and his communication with other children and the teacher was quite good, apart from some outburst now and then.

I was relieved about the news, but at the same time, I hoped nothing serious had happened, which would project Jo back to square one.

Some hypotheses were taking shape in my mind:

A trip to the sea side?

Had Bill turned up making some trouble?

The next week, a day before Jo's therapy appointment, the lady from the Social Services called and said that Jo would be attending the next session. There had been a consultation with the family about the return of Bill to the household.

The situation had been discussed, and in the end there seemed to be no major problem with

Bill returning. Even the children didn't oppose it, maybe because their mother was missing him and wanted him back.

Promises had been made about not drinking anymore, attending the AA meeting and so on. As usual, I had heard it all a thousand times before, and most of the time it didn't mean anything, and they were back in the pub in a week.

The good news was that Jo was alright and wanting to come back to the therapy room. I was relieved to know this because, with children, sometimes it is very difficult to reinstate a rapport after even a short break.

Children react in different ways, difficult to predict. On the other hand, it is never straightforward. You can expect a break of some sort now and then.

As always, I found myself thinking about the changes in Jo's life.

More than a change, it seemed to go back to the previous situation. How was Jo feeling about Bill returning to his home and in his life?

When Bill came to talk to me, he seemed sincere and a decent sort of man. However, people tend to lie to get what they want. Let's face it, they weren't on good terms. Jo resented him being there with them. He resented his behavior, his drinking habit, and now he was back. There must be a lot of apprehensions and negative feelings regarding this. On the other hand, children, I know, can change quickly given the right opportunity. In this case, they knew that Allison was very much in love with Bill and wanted him back. Concerning this, was Allison ready to include him in the family life, to trust him with her children and give him the opportunity to become close to them and them to him?

Of course, how can you trust someone who drinks?

Those are all questions that automatically come into the therapist's mind as well as preparing and hypothesizing for the next meeting.

When he came to the next session, Jo was smiling and in a good temper.

He went straight to the toy box and asked me: 'Where is the lock?'

"Oh," I said. "I thought you had forgotten the lock. You want to know where it is?"

"Yes," he continued. "That's what I said."

"Well," I answered. "It was there the last time I saw it."

"Who was playing with it?"

"Every kid who comes here likes to play with it once or twice," I responded.

He was now frantically going through the toys when he finally found it.

"Hurray!" He said.

"Hurray!" I replied. "You found it, well done!"

He looked at me quizzically and said:

"It wasn't such a big task. It isn't like I cracked the combination."

"Well, I don't know about that," I said. "Sometimes it must be like a nightmare to look in that box, everything is muddled together."

"Yes…" he said. "Already working on the lock, a bit of order would be nice."

"Yes." I agreed, "a bit of order would be nice. Who says that Jo? your mom?"

"My mom… she doesn't know what order is. My grandmother used to say that when she came to see us."

"What happened? She doesn't come to see you anymore?"

"No, she died three years ago," he said sadly.

"I am sorry, Jo." I left him working with the lock for a few minutes, to cope with the pain of what he had said in silence.

"Sure, you are missing your grannie!" I ventured. "How was she?"

He got tired now of working on the lock. He threw it aside and took a hen from the farm animal box. "It's a hen," he announced.

"Yes, it is," I confirmed.

"She's nice and caring. There are some animals on the farm who don't like her, like this one. There's a dog next to the hen."

"I see. The dog is not too pleased with the hen?"

"The hen likes to be free. The dog wants some order, control."

"I wonder why," I continued.

Now he was running the dog round the carpet in a frenetic mixture of jumps and stops.

"Control! Control! Control!" he repeated.

He got another toy out of the box and started to make a picture with them.

"Are you making a picture of the animals?" I asked.

He didn't answer, so I suggested, "a family?"

"Shush," he whispered. "It is not a family. This is the two-headed dinosaur... everyone is afraid of him."

"Everyone is afraid of the dinosaur?" I asked.

"Yes," he replied.

I was running now, and I couldn't stop.

"What makes everyone so scared?"

"You would be scared if you saw a dinosaur!"

"I suppose I would be scared if I saw one. But I am not likely to see one, am I?" I asked.

"Who knows," he answered, still placing the dinosaur almost on top of the group of animals.

I carried on. "They seem to know him, and they are not scared?"

"They will be in a minute when they go to bed," he replied.

"So, the dinosaur scares them when they are in bed?" I asked him to confirm.

"Yes, it does" he confirmed.

"I wonder if they are asleep when the dinosaur comes in and scares them," I asked.

"Sometimes they are asleep; sometimes they are not sleeping because they are afraid of the dinosaur," he replied.

"Does it come into their dreams, to scare them?" I asked.

"I don't know," he replied and seemed genuine, "Maybe," he concluded.

The buzz of my receptionist told me that Jo's mother had arrived, and she was waiting for him.

"I know," he said as if he had read my thoughts, "time to go, time to go."

He left me with that puzzle to sort out. The dinosaur comes to them at night, when they are in bed, and it scares them. And the lock? He just forgot about it.

Children dream about frightening things and imagine it is happening in real life, but also, I have to consider that the dinosaur might be a person, a motivation, an action, anything that would bring apprehension to an already disturbed child. Then there was the dog, usually a friendly, faithful animal. Was the dog there to protect them from the dinosaur, even though he wanted order and control? Or was the dinosaur pretending to be a scary animal because he was seeking power and control?

Sometimes, with children, you will never solve the puzzle; it is all part of a greater picture. At times they keep the solution for themselves, and at the same time they work out the issues by themselves, almost as if they were saying; you are here to help me, I am not going to tell you everything about myself; in fact, I shall keep it for myself. At the same time, you are useful to me, and I will know you are only guessing.

There is no problem with that if it is beneficial to the child in the long run. After all, we are here to help to solve their issues, and if that means frustration for the therapist, well, it is just a part of the job.

I genuinely wanted to understand the child, to be able to help him in any possible way. I can make all the conjecture and hypotheses I like, but in the end, the reality is what counts and the result.

Jo was doing remarkably well. His behavior had improved, so had his social skills. Reports from the school were coming in saying that he had improved so much, and he didn't even need any supervision during the school hours.

He was better at playing with other children and even though sometimes he liked to stay on his own, he did not have a single fight with other pupils for a long time. I was very pleased with the news; a change of behavior was a sign of his improvement. But what interested me more than anything else was Jo on the inside, not so much the outside.

Spring was coming, and the weather was improving greatly. I could not stop to wonder how long the therapy would last and whether anything else might happen to disturb the proceeding of the therapy itself. It is only natural that the issues that arise will reflect on our own lives, particularly our childhood experiences. Transference is helpful if you know it is taking place. I got used to it, in fact, if anything, it helps me at times.

I could remember when I was four years old and my mother was taking me to the primary school, then run by nuns. I hated that place, and I didn't want to go there. I cried all morning, but as usual my mother was having none of it and decided that I had to go to the nuns.

She took my hand, and she was pulling me with all her strength towards the convent.

Even at that age, I remember having been quite strong and determined to get my own way. There was a long wall on the road that took us to the place, and under the wall a ravine and the sea.

She was trying to scare me, pushing me towards the ravine and at the same time holding me tightly. I started to hit her on the head with my lunch pack, quickly and strongly. Suddenly, the plastic corner of the pack hit her on the forehead, and she started bleeding.

Then she pulled me back on the road and walked quickly and angrily towards home. She didn't speak to me for 3 or 4 days. She never tried again to take me to the nuns.

The composure of the parents will in time reflect on the children of course. Parenting is a very difficult and demanding job. Nevertheless, we are all human and can make mistakes, even though we should think hard before we form a pattern of action which can hurt a child.

Personally, I never stopped analyzing her behavior, even when I was very young. Being the youngest, I was the only child who believed her and every time she said she was going to leave us, I used to run after her pleading: 'mom, please don't do it, we love you!' Nobody else came with me, and I was so surprised at the coldness of my siblings. Didn't they care? And why did my mother go to the extent of walking out, pretending she was going to leave us, usually after a futile argument with her daughters?

That went on for years; she never spoke about it again. I never asked her why. I wished I had, later in life when I was growing up, and she was getting old. I think I pushed all those things into my subconscious and it never surfaced until now.

Is this why I am writing about these experiences at this time?

CHAPTER 7

Next session, when Jo came, I could sense something had happened. He was more nervous than usual, and his disruptive behavior had come to the surface again.

He wasn't very cooperative, and he just wanted to slam on the floor pretending he was sleeping.

If I said anything he wouldn't answer, or he would just groan like an animal and pretend he was having a fit.

I left him there for a while before I started asking him some questions.

Trust, I thought, was established a few sessions before, so I felt strongly about it and began to ask him gently.

"Jo, I feel something must have happened to you during this week. I am interested in knowing what had happened to you, can you tell me please?"

After a long silence, he replied, "there's nothing to say."

"Well," I insisted, 'sometimes we all feel that way, and it's just nice and helpful to talk about it. You know, you can tell me anything, anything at all. Do you remember the rules we established the first time I saw you?"

"Yes, yes, I remember," he said. He was finally, after half an hour, coming to his senses and willing to cooperate.

"Can I draw?" He said. "Of course," I replied, giving him paper and color that were always at a short distance from me.

"Here, feel free to start drawing when you are ready."

I noticed he was drawing quickly and intensively. There was a classroom and desks and pupils sat at desks; it was quite a competent drawing, considering his age. A boy was half hidden under his desk; he had a sort of angry face while the boy next to him was laughing and pointing a big finger at the boy who was hidden under the desk.

It was an easy picture to interpret. Something had happened in the classroom, and he didn't want to talk about it. Children can be cruel to each other at school; bullying is very common, especially in a special school for children with learning difficulties.

"I see," I said, "would you like to talk about what happened there, Jo?"

"No, I don't want to talk about it." I left it at that.

"What else has happened Jo, during the last week?"

He told me in his confused way that someone comes into the bedroom, looking for something under the carpet, and everywhere else in the room. He has many arms, and suddenly he disappears. He told his mother about it, but she didn't believe him.

Time passes quickly when you talk, I thought. It was time to end the session, and it had been a very fruitful one, lots of statements and material to work on. For instance, the man in the bedroom, what is the belief that no one trusted or believed his story? Finding something under the carpet begins from a sense of pride, the growing self.

The Social Services canceled our next appointment. Bill had been found dead outside the local pub. There was an investigation pending; they would give me more information later.

I sensed a long break in Jo's therapy again.

Allison telephoned me the day after and told me the tragic story again. She was very upset and told me Jo would be unable to come to the therapy room for a while.

As a counseling psychologist, I find myself often in a situation like this: the parent or parents are aware that the helper already has the information from the Social Services and police if they are concerned about the welfare of the child.

Too early to jump to conclusions, I thought. Often, when you think you reach the target, all of a sudden the therapy could go back to square one, without an explanation or a motive; or, worse, it could be interrupted for health reasons, by the parents, the Social Services and as in this case by the police.

After all, there was an investigation pending. I decided not to get involved with the bureaucracy.

Somehow, when you try to interfere with them, you always come out worse off. Like all bureaucracies, once the mechanism starts and files move from one desk to another, it is very difficult to halt. I discuss the case in supervision, and I feel confident in doing so, but at the end of the day, the decision is mine and nobody else's.

There was a certain coming together feeling, with Jo's therapy, for the first time since we started. I felt satisfied with the positive movement in Jo's behavior.

There were many things still to deal with: the lack of concentration, so often visible in children who have been neglected by the parents or caregivers in the first two years of their lives; the anger that is still lodged in the child's psyche needing just a little disappointment to trigger it; the impaired ability to create lasting interrelationship with other children; the failures of recall. All these are hypotheses and thoughts the therapist goes through, during the length of the therapy.

What was the significance of the lock? The locked self, finding out, discovery, getting to know people, getting out of imprisonment, rebelling, plan, archetypes, feelings, feelings of inadequacy, anger management, discover the truth.

He once said to me: "I will find out about me, about you, about people!" Find out what? I thought.

Who's the man in the bedroom, looking for hidden things under the carpet? Or is it a fantasy? I had a deep thought.

Is the under-carpet his subconscious, wanting to come up and free him from his prison? Is it the locked self?

Comparing Jo's case with those of other patients like Gemma, for instance, is almost impossible. Every case is different and unique, just like all of us, human beings.

To be able to go further with the therapy, you must almost lose the sense of self and focus completely and entirely on the patient.

Connecting, disconnecting is something that every therapist and psychologist must do, and a very experienced practitioner can do that as a matter of course. That doesn't mean that he's not focusing, but the opposite. Otherwise, he could not cope with other children who came into therapy with so many different problems and issues. In an ideal world, every child has a happy and healthy upbringing.

Life today shows us that it is not always possible because inevitable conditions of life happen.

Marriage splits, of course, don't help and nor do many other factors; for instance, drug addiction, prostitution, Aids, change of lifestyle, violence, abuse, just to mention a few, which make the family's life disrupted and difficult, or even make it impossible for children to cope and live with them.

Not only a dysfunctional family but neglect, lack of means to provide for the child's needs, even murder in Jo's case!

I just hoped the latter would not interfere with his therapy. Involvement with the police is necessary of course in this case, but it could end the therapy.

The lack of information on the matter made me think that none of the parties wanted to get involved with that aspect, now that Jo's improvement was evident, and they were very happy to wait for further developments.

A month after, Jo could come to the playroom again.

"I want to play with the sand tray!" he commanded as soon as he got into the therapy room. "You would like to have a go with the sand tray?" I repeated. "Be my guest; you know where it is." He nodded and went to get the box of toys first and positioned it near the sand tray.

He sat on the floor, next to the sand tray. I sat next to him watching every movement he made. From the box, he dragged out the combination lock and several other toys including some farm animals, wild animals, some soldiers, and cars.

"You have a great mix of people, animals, and toys!" I said.

"Yes," he agreed. "Animals, people, cars, and soldiers," he continued, pulling out a single soldier, "First" he announced, "the lock." And with a quick movement of his hands, he buried the lock in the sand.

"That's it!" he shouted after he was satisfied with his action. He kept pressing the sand down, to make sure the combination lock didn't come up to the surface.

"I see, you have buried the lock," I verified showing my surprise. "Yes. I buried the lock," he replied.

"I thought you wanted to crack the combination." I asked. "Yes, I do. I have buried it for now," he answered.

"I see. You still want to find the last two numbers."

He didn't answer. He started to bury some farm animals, a red car, and a soldier. All this was done in silence. I didn't want to interfere or interrupt his action.

Whatever he was doing, it was evident to me that he was trying to get something out of his system and it seemed to be working well.

The burying of the combination lock made me think a lot about the symbolic interpretation.

After session upon session, dedicated to cracking the two final numbers, he was dismissing it and trying to cancel it forever.

He did say for now, but did he mean it? Maybe he was fed up with playing with it, or he found it too difficult to solve, and he was too proud to admit it. Probably he didn't find out any numbers at all, and he was trying to fool himself and me. There was an opportunity to challenge him there, but I decided to wait and see the end of the play. I was there to accept whatever he was doing and see any results produced by his actions. He kept playing with the sand tray now and talking to me, now and then.

"I have buried the soldier," he shouted again. "I must make sure he doesn't come out anymore!"

He was hitting the sand with his fists as if he wanted to rain heavy blows on the soldier he had buried.

"You are making sure he will not come out anymore?"

"Yes, that's what I am doing," he answered me promptly with an annoyed attitude.

"What does he want anyway?" I thought that would be a good moment to intervene and ask him again about the man in his bedroom; or was it a hallucination?

"Yes," I continued. "What does he want and why does he keep coming out at night in your bedroom, looking for something under the carpet? What is he looking for?"

"I don't know!" He said. "Last night he didn't look. He just sat on my bed looking at me and then he jumped up in the air and disappeared."

"What does he look like?" I asked. "Don't know,'" he repeated. "He doesn't have a face; it's all black and dark and, he's got more than two arms."

A kind of gigantic octopus, I thought to myself. The description of the man was getting more precise now, but also more surreal.

I was quite relieved now because it sounded like a dream, a nightmare, a vivid imagination of something alien, who would make his life interesting and exciting at the same time. He was probably a figure of a computer game or a creepy movie that he shouldn't have been watching.

Somehow, I knew it had to have a link with his life and his psyche. Children don't make up stories for nothing; there's always a reason for that.

"He has more than two arms, but you don't know exactly how many. Is that what you mean, Jo?" He looked at me with an uncertain expression in his eyes.

"Too dark to tell you," He replied. "He doesn't have wings, but he can fly.' I just thought how much I remembered in my youth about fantasy and imagination. The fairy coming flying, all dressed in white with large wings, in an incredible misty luminous area. In this case, the figure was the opposite: dark, black, no wings, not evangelical, but quite disturbing, even though, as I remember, some figures can be black and prophetic, for instance representing death and gloom.

It's all part of the phenomenological stance of our life. Normally we are aware of our position in life; we tend to keep a foot firmly on the ground. Sometimes, though, we let our imaginations wander, and anything could happen. Children are more prone to this, and in a way, it's a reminder to us that fantasy still exists in our minds. It's a little bit like the skeletons dancing over the linen cupboard by my bedroom window when I was a child. I still can remember it vividly, and it will be with me forever. To this day I can't tell if it really happened. Was it a dream or not? It's nice sometimes to remember our childhood. It can help us to think that we are still able to lose ourselves in a fantasy tour. The bonus is also that it helps us to understand our children if only we listen to them and have the time to do so.

"How did that make you feel, Jo?" I asked him directly.

This could be a very difficult question to answer. He looked at me intensely and then said, "Frightened at first and then relieved."

 "Relieved?" I was surprised by his expression. "Yes," he continued. "I wasn't frightened anymore, quite happy to have seen him doing that."

I was a bit confused by his answer. "Jo, to make sure I understand what you mean, you felt frightened first and then you felt relieved, by knowing that you were not frightened anymore. Is that what you mean?" "Yes," He affirmed. "Like I knew him, I got used to him."

Jo is internalizing the feeling with the imagination, I assumed. He's probably starting the process of getting rid of him; in any case, not a regression but progress.

I was quite pleased with what he was saying. "That's a good thing, Jo, you weren't scared anymore, but aren't you curious to know who he really is?"

To my surprise, he announced: "I am going to carry on playing with the sand tray, in fact, I am going to bury that nasty dinosaur with everything else and say goodbye!" he announced, seeming satisfied with his decision.

"Well, you have been burying everything this morning Jo, but tell me, I am going to ask a question that most of the kids who come here find helpful. If you wanted to save one of the objects, people, animals you have buried, which one would it be?"

He looked at me thoughtfully. Then, with a quick, almost frenetic motion took out from the sand a silver object.

I first saw its shining metallic side coming out of the sand, and then the black dial of the combination came to the surface once again.

Yes, it was the old combination lock un-buried. Surprisingly, I was relieved by the choice; there was still work to do with it.

This showed me a sense of acute determination uncommon in kids of his age. A sense of tenacity and diligence.

Time was up for the session; we had come a long way. The journey ahead was still long, but possibly I noted a glimmer of hope.

Children often let things go quickly, especially if they are difficult or boring.

They can start an activity and then immediately go on to the next one, completely forgetting the previous one. Jo was not like that; he was determined to finish the activity he started, even if it presented some uncommon difficulties. With his attitude, he was showing me pride and diligence, which was the strength of his character. He showed me a sense of self-determination to succeed. His confidence and self-esteem had improved along with his interrelationship with the family and the school. He had become more relaxed during the session and reports from the teacher were very positive. There were some areas of his character to be worked on still, and in need of more attention, but the improvement had been a major factor in Jo's therapy.

CHAPTER 8

Allison rang me up, saying she wanted to speak to me urgently.

It was a long time since our last conversation, and I was intrigued by the reason why she wanted to talk to me.

What was she going to talk about? During the meeting, she apologized for not being able to speak to me sooner.

"As you probably know, a lot is going on, and I didn't want to make it any more difficult for Jo and you."

She said it all in one breath. "You must be wondering what the reasons for all this are, and I want to put it right."

I told her to explain further and that I didn't know anything about what she was trying to tell me.

She looked older than I remember, and she seemed to be sort of harassed, as though she was afraid somebody had been following her. "I am so happy seeing Jo blossoming. I am eternally grateful to you doc," she told me emotionally. "Early days yet," I replied.

I didn't want to build her hopes too much; children can change suddenly, and unhelpful behavior can return.

Environment and families play a big part in this and there's nothing the therapist can say or do. "Well, he's now the boy I always wanted him to be. He's like a little man in the family. I can't believe it!"

I looked at her trying to gather some compassion for the woman who was probably the cause of it all.

"Jo has always been like that." I managed to say in the kindest possible way I could.

She looked at me, and suddenly her expression became sad and thoughtful. "We are all confused and sad. What? Bill, murdered? I still can't believe it."

She was tearful now. "I only saw him an hour before, and he was looking sober and relaxed. Of course, as always, he couldn't wait to go to the pub but, dispatching drugs? No, that was not Bill! He got mixed up with the wrong crowd. Some shifty character in that pub and living in a council tower block, where we live, how can we avoid them? I myself was approached several times to sell stuff. I always told my kids to be careful and not to get talking to anybody in our building. Bill never listened to me, though I warned him many times. That was him, didn't listen much and now look at what has happened."

I remained completely surprised and confused by it all, "I am sorry," I said. "I am a bit confused. What exactly happened?"

"I thought you knew everything already, I am sorry," she said. "I thought Jo told you everything. After Bill's murder, the police came many times looking for drugs in our flat or anything they could find. They didn't tell us anything; they just came in and did all they wanted. The children were upset, and I had to get in touch with the Social Services because I couldn't handle the situation anymore. Bill and I hardly saw each other for the last two months, even though, I suspect, he came to our flat two or three times at night. Jo told me a confused story about somebody being in his bedroom. I never went to the pub drinking with him, he always went alone and, apparently that's where he met those people who gave him the stuff to sell. The police told me the trafficking must have been going on for quite some time. It was well known to the police, and they started to watch the pub and follow Bill, to catch him while he was selling the stuff. So they say, but I don't believe them."

She rested for a while. "Bill wasn't like that, my idea is that Bill refused to do what they wanted him to do and they killed him because they thought he had informed the police and had given them their names. Bill was not a grass."

I was left astonished by the revelation:

"Thank you for telling me this Allison. I was completely unaware all this was taking place. As you know, I am not a policeman, and usually, I don't get involved with this kind of things. How do you feel about all this? It seems to me, it's a very difficult matter to cope with," I told her trying to be as empathic as I could.

"At the moment, I am trying to cope the best I can, but I am afraid of the people who killed Bill because they know me, and somehow they think I was involved in all of this. I have been followed and threatened by them. They think I am hiding some of their stuff and came looking for that in our flat. I am sure somebody was following me even today, coming here."

Immediately the man in Jo's bedroom, searching under the carpet, came to my mind.

"I see." I responded. "This sounds dangerous and cannot be underestimated. What have you done about it?" I asked.

"What can I do about it?" she repeated. "Go to the police? They will start all over again, and they'll think I was involved as well. I am sure they are already thinking like that. There's very little I can do about it!"

I thought she was probably becoming paranoid after all this happening.

"Allison, you have been going through a very difficult time, it's only natural now to feel unsafe and threatened." Allison's confession unsettled me for a while. There's nothing worse than fear, real or imagined. Fear can physically hurt and make your life a misery. There was also nothing I could say to improve her situation. After all, her fears could be a reality, for all I knew. I decided just to listen.

After an hour, when she left, she looked relieved and calmer. She downloaded everything onto me, and obviously, she felt better. I was glad to know more about the incident. I only had bits of information from Jo, which turned out to be real, but I was unaware of the whole story. It seemed to be more complicated than I had imagined. The investigation was very much at a preliminary stage because when drugs are involved, it's only natural that the police want to find out a lot more about the trafficking involved in the area and outside the area. There was much more going on in Jo's council estate; it was renowned for drugs, delinquency, and prostitution.

When Jo came to the next session, he seemed to be quiet, happy and relaxed. He told me he wanted to play with the finger paint. As always, I encouraged him to do just that, while I would observe him and interact with him if I found the opportunity and felt the need to do so. The thing to be painted today was a representation of all the family, including brother, sisters, mother, and grandmother, connected to each other in different ways. Some of them were united by sharp lines, others by dots, but though all of them seemed to be united by something, and eventually the picture took the shape of a circle with a big round black space in the middle, which appeared to spoil the happy painting somehow and did not have a connection to the outer circle.

"What is the black dot in the middle Jo?" I questioned him.

"It's the murderer," he said.

Without flinching an eyelid, "Bill's murderer?" I enquired.

"Who else?" Jo responded in a matter-of-fact way.

"I suppose it makes you wonder," I responded, hoping for some more information about it: "It's not every day that murder happens close to you!"

He looked sad now and continued. "Yes, it had to happen to us."

I kept thinking that it must have affected him more than he was letting on. "What do you think had happened?" I asked.

"Bill must have known a lot about the people in the estate who sell drugs," he replied.

"Good thinking Jo. What about letting the police and the investigation solve the mystery?"

"Fine, I just know that's what has happened."

"Ok, Jo, but let's focus on you. How do you feel today?"

He looked as if he was going to ignore me: "I am going to play with my lock today."

I was annoyed by his dismissive answer. Then I asked: "About the lock, I was going to ask you Jo, any progress with it?"

He looked at me and then he said. "Fine, I am doing fine. Two numbers to go as I said before. Why do you want to know?"

"No problem, I just wanted to know if I could help you at all."

"Are you saying you know them?"

'No, sorry, I don't know the combination. What are the two numbers you have already found?" I asked him. He repeated the numbers which I knew already. As he was busy working, I looked in my diary where I put the combinations of my bike's new lock. To my surprise, I discovered that they were the same numbers. If anything happens, I thought, I can reveal the whole combination because, obviously, the numbers of the same type of lock are all the same, "That's good news, Jo. You are nearly there. There are only two numbers to find out."

"Yes and, I don't want any help from you, thank you very much."

"I wasn't going to help you, Jo, I just want you to find the combination quickly so that we can concentrate on other things too," I said. He looked at me and didn't answer. I knew, in the end, he would do as he liked.

The time had come to end the session. Jo threw everything in the box quickly and left without saying anything, a little later than usual.

There was nothing left for me to do than think about the content of the therapy session. There was new evidence about Bill's murder, that's what I understood during Jo's session. The lock came back as fresh as ever, progress was slow, but he was determined to find the missing digits. This gave me a good insight into his character.

He was not really trying to find the numbers; he was trying to find himself, during all the things happening in his life, in his mind. There was a new sense of family bonding, and that is only natural in a period of crisis. Strangely, there wasn't any presence of fear in Jo's behavior, and that was a very positive outcome. I felt a bit apprehensive about the fact that he was getting involved in the crime and trying to solve it. It's not unusual for children to fantasize about police crimes, especially if it involves them and the family.

Next session Jo was very talkative. He told me they went to the seaside for the weekend.

"Who took you there?" I asked. "Bill's friend Ted took us there, his mom's new friend now."

I don't believe it! I thought, Allison is repeating the same mistake. I pretended I was alright with it. "That's great; can you tell me all about it? Please, I'd like to know." He started to tell me about all the games and activities they played together during the break. Obviously, I didn't expect the whole list of events, especially from somebody like Jo, who could jump from one thing to another and leave out the bits necessary for a complete picture to be formed.

"Did anybody ask Ted if he knew anything about what happened to Bill?" He did not answer, which is what I meant by saying that his communication was limited.

"Spring is coming, what are we going to do today, Jo?" I suggested at the beginning of the next session.

"I want to play, play, play," he voiced.

"That is not a bad idea, as always you can play with whatever you like. What do you fancy today?"

"There is something we did which I'd like to do again. It was something about the future, the magic ball. Where is it?"

For me, one of the most important things in therapy is to empower the child in the playroom. Even the choice of a game can be very difficult, when a child has been psychologically deprived of most things, which are basic but very important for healthy growth to occur. It seems a little thing, but it took months of work for Jo to arrive at this stage.

He was referring to a drawing we did together a few months back. It was a simple drawing of three crystal spheres, equivalent to three wishes for the future. "Very well, I will go and find it," I replied.

A few seconds later, having looked in the folder where I kept his stuff, I was back with the task.

"Here it is Jo," I gave him the drawing. He took it without saying thank you. "Three wishes for the future, Jo."

He was digging through the box to find the colors he wanted to use. There were many types of colors, felt tip pens, pencils, finger paints and others. He started to draw quickly in the first sphere. "This is the house where I want to live in the future," he told me. "It's a big house, with a garden near the sea. There are five bedrooms upstairs and a play area in the loft, where we all can go to play during the winter. During the summer, we can play on the beach. The garden is full of flowers, and there are many windows overlooking the sea. There is a big kitchen where mum cooks, and we all help to prepare dinner. We all work in the garden, and there's a man helping us. He doesn't drink, and we are all happy together. There aren't any noises at night, and nobody comes into the house because it's ours. During the day we go and play in the sand, we swim together and splash each other in the sea."

It was a very primitive drawing. Jo wasn't very good at drawing, but with a bit of imagination I could follow the story.

"It sounds very good," I said, encouraging him to carry on. He looked for a few seconds at the crystal ball and then started to draw in the second wish. There were some odd short black pencil stubs here and there, which I related to his darkest moments of isolation. He drew a cross on each of them as if to stop them from happening again. I was relieved when I was told that they had gone. "It was to prevent them from happening again," he said. The third one, I thought, was an abstract one made of scribbles, dots, lines, and blobs. Impossible to give them an interpretation, even though it's always best not to interpret. The patient knows best, and he or she will give an interpretation when they are ready to do so. It's often possible to encourage them in that task or to give options now and then if necessary. During all that, I seemed to be able to recognize a corner of the therapy room, but it was all confused between scribbles and blobs. I was waiting for his explanation, without prompts if possible. It took quite a while and, I was worried because the end of the session was approaching. I didn't want to leave out such an important part of the session. Nevertheless, I waited patiently, and I was rewarded for that.

"This is about me, you, and the playroom. Me inside, from the beginning till now."

I was listening actively and showing all my interest, paying full attention to what he was saying to me. He carried on explaining:

"This blob in the corner, it's me when I first came into the playroom. It's dark and unfriendly," he said. These are very precious pieces of information, given by a patient of young age at a certain point of therapy, and they are very valuable. The unfriendly note stuck in my mind. That is how he perceived the session, even though everything was made to look warm and friendly and yet the sense of this little kid was that it looked dark and unfriendly, which made him feel that the environment was awkward and somber. There was a continuation of patterns in his explanation, which as a whole made a lot of sense and described exactly how he felt at the given time. Expressing your feelings is never easy, particularly at that age. I thought Jo was coping remarkably well and he showed his progress mentally and physically. The session was coming to an end, and I didn't want to put more pressure on him.

The work in this session was done, and I felt relieved and pleased with the results. There were of course issues to cope with in future sessions. The involvement in crime, and consequent issues with the police and the Social Services, who were just looking for proof to be able to separate them. With all that happening, even if it was outside the therapy, they were producing consequences. In my early work with victims of a crime relating to serious investigations, I learned a lot about the reactions and consequences of family involvement. Children are very much affected by that, even if they are not involved personally. They tend to internalize the problem and most of the time they blame themselves, even if the connection is minimal. Crimes in the family are more common than we think.

CHAPTER 9

Domestic violence in the household involving children is very common. I remember dealing with a child in a murder case very similar to this one. A woman who lived next door to the child in question was murdered. The child didn't know the particulars of course, but she knew somebody had been killed next door. The girl was a friend of her son, and she became withdrawn and scared about going to school, sleeping alone and even refused to participate in any activities and play during the school hours. At home, she became silent and irrational. She had panic attacks for a long time after the murder, paranoid and traumatic experiences.

I was aware that there was going to be a break in Jo's therapy during the summer months. Nothing had been said, but eventually there was going to be a break caused by a summer holiday for kids who needed to get away from the city and don't have the resources which allows them to do that, like for instance holiday camps and other institutions. There was still time to continue our work before the summer months, and I was going to prepare Jo for the break. I didn't want to undo the work we had already done. There was a period of quietness and silence after the last session, we had reached a pinnacle point of the therapy itself, but we weren't out of the woods, so to speak.

The news that a man had been arrested for Bill's murder reached me through the local Press. The idea that it was going to cause further panic to the family, as the sordid affair continued, disturbed me a lot.

How was Jo going to take the news? Was it going to unsettle him further? Would it be a relief, or would it bring chaos and fear? Allison would certainly have been affected by it. I hoped this would be in a positive way because the police arrested the culprit. The paranoid effect that she was experiencing would terminate, and it would positively influence the kids. Too early to make a judgment, I thought. In the next session, I would have a clearer idea of Jo's state of mind relating to the possible conclusion of Bill's murder.

The day before Jo's session, I received a call from Allison, Jo's mother, telling me that he couldn't come to therapy that week. I asked her to tell me the reason for him not attending the appointment, and she replied that it had something to do with the Social Services adjournment. "Can you explain further?" I asked. It's not for me to get involved in private matters, but knowing about Bill's news, I suspected it was to do with the police, and some issues on confidentiality could be involved in that decision.

"It has to do with Bill's case, and the police want to ask Jo about certain things he said. Of course, the Social Services will be present at the interview. The man arrested is our neighbor, Ted, she told me, sounding very upset. "I see," I answered. Feeling a bit concerned about the interference of the police with Jo's therapy. "I hope it's not going to be a long interruption.

Will you keep me informed, please? I am concerned about the effect that this will have on Jo's progress."

"So am I" she answered promptly. "The Social Services lady told me that she was going to keep you up to date. Thank you, doc and goodbye."

She sounded very sincere and cooperative. I was pleased with that, but, I couldn't help thinking that what they say and what they do sometimes are two very different things.

Counseling a child is a very complex procedure. Parents and careers can lie if it suits them. They are always afraid of compromising themselves, by saying something which could take the kids away from them. Children never lie, unless they are protecting someone, or they feel responsible for something that happened in their family. Parents, most of the time, keep some information to themselves for the reason I have already explained. In this case, I thought she sounded sincere, but there was something she didn't tell me, I had a gut feeling about it.

This last break gave me a bit of time to think about Jo's therapy, his progress, and future interventions. At the same time, I could focus more on other kids I was seeing, particularly a young girl, whose therapy was ending soon.

When one of my patients, Gemma, came in she was as cheerful as ever. The changes she had undergone were significant indeed; from a withdrawn shy child, she had blossomed into a sparkling young girl, full of life and mischief.

When she started therapy almost a year ago, she couldn't speak to anybody. She would sit in a corner like a wounded animal. Communicating with her was difficult. She would hardly eat anything, and she would spend hours in silence, sobbing.

It was all her own doing; she worked very hard to take on the changes that now are there to see. She was suffering from anorexia, paranoid hallucination and physical pains. Her clinician had given up on her. She was almost on the brink of depression when I started to see her. It had been just by chance because her therapist was having some serious problems herself, and she was admitted to a hospital far away from where she lived.

Gemma's referral notes recorded deep rooted mental issues. I had worked with patients with anorexia in the past, in conjunction with medical supervision. Who would check the physical side of the patient's progress?

I accepted Gemma's referral and therapy started immediately, the week after she called me. Strangely enough, the first time I saw her, I thought that the little girl had potential to get better. Something in her told me that she had a lot of inner strength, and would collaborate with me, given the right ambiance and the right approach. Today, I must admit my feelings were right, and Gemma was responding to the therapy well, to the point that she had developed a sense of humor that was unique.

The journey was not easy, especially for her. I was determined not to give up on her and give her the opportunity to grow. There was a time when it was very difficult to make a judgment on her progress, but for me, the main part of the therapy was not to let her go, and to empower her, to make small changes in her life. This is what I saw of Gemma at the end of her therapy. It isn't particularly easy ending the rapport with a patient like Gemma, who had attachment issues and who got attached tightly to our working relationship. Concluding with her occupied the last four sessions. We discussed it and decided together that a good time to finish would be just before the summer holiday.

She went through many painful emotions during the last two sessions. It was necessary to give her time to understand that it was a good decision, for her and her life. By the time of her last session, Gemma had become less emotional and more concrete. She had realized that it was time to go and face the world on her own, with the help of the people around her, family and friends, who were very supportive and loving. I was struggling to find the right way to do it and what to say. I opted for a kind of positive and progressive one:

"Tell me, Gemma, what will you be doing next week at this time?"

She muttered, "Who is taking my place?" There was still some sadness in her voice.

"I don't know yet, now it is vacant." I answered as a matter of fact. "By the way," I continued. "Nobody can take your place. I mean no one can be you. There's only one of you, you are unique and special."

"I like that! Will you think of me?" She moaned with a trembling voice.

"I will, I think of you and every kid who has been here with me, in the therapy room." I answered as sincerely as I could. "I want to keep you in my memory as you are now and think of all the good work we have done together, in this room and how you've changed. I am very proud of you."

It was time to go, and she left smiling and full of promises. "I will write you during the summer holiday," she told me.

"Thank you, Gemma, 'I'd like to know how you are getting on. Time will come when you won't write anymore. Don't worry about that, it's a normal process, but if anytime you'd like to get in touch with me, you know where I am," I continued. This is what I tell every patient in the last session.

Patients, particularly kids and adolescents, like to know that they can get in touch with the therapist any time after the therapy ends. It's like a safety net, and they like to have that choice if they need it.

It is a long, painful journey and unconsciously, they don't want to go back where they started from. Personally, I don't mind giving them that possibility even though I don't work with transference, I am not their father, and they are not my children. Empowerment is the most useful tool for helping children, and I make sure they understand this at a very early stage in the therapy.

 In the case of Gemma, she responded very well, and now she oversees her feelings and her choices. Most parents try to do their best for their children, but they are not trained psychologists or psychotherapists. Even though they are concerned for the welfare and upbringing of their children, they can make mistakes and continue to make them. They are not aware of the problems a kid goes through at an early stage of their childhood.

The therapist, most of the time, finds that he or she must counsel the parents not only the child. Everything the children tell you in the therapy room is, of course, confidential; they can say what they would like you to tell their parents or caregivers to improve rapport. You would be surprised to know how little talk there is between parents and their children.

When you tell the parents: "your son says you are putting too much pressure on him," or "your daughter said you were not telling her the truth" etc., they look at you in amazement, as if their children don't have the right to ask for anything, that doesn't belong to the position of being a child and what a child should say or do according to their perspective. Then, of course, you realize there is something not working in the family, no communication, some sort of abuse and so on.

To abuse a child doesn't mean that you must beat them up, since abuse could be psychological rather than physical. The silent sort is the most common. It is difficult to spot and difficult to deal with because most of the time the family don't realize what they are doing to their children.

It was a long break for Jo, which lasted about a month. When he came back, I was apprehensive about the result. I hoped we weren't going back to square one, I thought, looking at him coming back into the playroom. We had made a lot of progress, and it would be awful to start all over again, for Jo's sake and my own.

I wanted to know what had happened in that long period, the full story. I decided not to ask and wait for him to tell me voluntarily. Obviously, it was just what he was thinking too because while he was working on the lock again, he kept looking at me as much as to say: "Don't you want to know? I know you want to know. Why don't you ask me?"

I felt a little cruel in doing this to him, but the aim of the therapy must be entirely focused on the patient, not what has happened to him or her or the therapist's curiosity about it, even if they are interwoven into each other. It wasn't a long time to wait before he deliberated:

"Ted, our neighbor, has been arrested. The police came and took him away last week."

I already knew it, but I wanted him to tell me. Ted, their neighbor and potentially Allison's new boyfriend, was involved in the murder.

"How is that possible, Jo?" I asked him.

"He was the one who came in our flat looking for things under the bed and carpet. He had Bill's keys," he continued.

It was clear now; Jo hadn't imagined the whole episode: they weren't hallucinations, dreams or nightmares; Ted's was in Jo's bedroom looking for the rest of the drugs. "What happened after that, Jo?" I continued.

"The policeman came to the school when I was getting ready to go home and asked me if I wanted to help with the inquiry. I said yes," Jo continued.

"When my mother came to collect me she was upset and had a go at him. I said I wanted to help, and so she asked him to tell her what that was all about," he said with a very excited voice.

"The policeman said it would only take half an hour and nobody would see us. We went with him, and he took us into a room where men, standing next to each other were staring at me. He said they wouldn't see me or hear us. Then he asked me if I recognized one of them. They were all wearing hoods. He stopped for a while catching his breath, I couldn't see their faces properly, but there was no doubt. I recognized him straight away. He was wearing the same black tracksuit, the third in the line; I was sure it was him. I told the policeman, and he said, thank you. Then we went back home."

"Didn't you recognize it was your neighbor, in the line Jo?" I asked him.

"Yes, I did then. My mother kept saying; "are you sure Jo? Are you sure?" "Yes, I am sure." She was upset, but I couldn't help her. It was him, and the police went to his house and found a lot of stuff which belonged to Bill," he continued.

I was relieved to hear that there was a proper investigation conducted by the police and evidence had been gathered. At the same time, I was annoyed to know that the police had not been following the Social Service's advice and accosted a child without the proper authorization. The fact that the mother was there was a point in their favor, as was the outcome, which I hoped would close the case permanently.

"Alright Jo, I am impressed by your handling of the case and solving it for them, but now let's concentrate on you and your feelings, how do you feel about all the things now?"

"I feel fine; I am happy, mum feels better too. She's not angry anymore, and she cooks good food for us."

"That can only be good!" I told him. "Happiness and food are very important. Would you like to draw a picture now about your feelings and what you are going to do next? School is about to close for the summer months," He did. He drew diligently and passionately, in his usual abstract way. There were still some spaces to be filled, but the result was satisfactory and revealing.

"I feel fine," he responded in an adult-like way. "I feel as if we are going somewhere and I can start to be happy."

I was happy too with his progress for now, and I was thinking about his future. I understood there were things to be dealt with if Jo was to grow as an individual. There were gaps in the system; the slowness of thought hadn't reached its full potential. His abstract thinking needed to be improved. He still had some anger episodes, and he had wet himself occasionally. I was looking at him while he was drawing, and I could see a little boy who had come a long way in the journey of self- discovery, but still had some distance to cover.

Perhaps I was too severe with him, I reflectively asked myself. Maybe Jo was ready to take the remaining journey by himself. It was a risk I didn't want to take. I dismissed the idea and got ready to carry on the work in the usual way.

Allison came to speak to me a week later, all breathy and excited. They had received an invitation from a relative, and they were leaving for Devon next weekend. It was a sudden decision taken together.

"Jo wanted to come to the playroom, but there were things to do and prepare. I have decided to come myself and explain the situation personally and properly."

In English, we say: "you could have knocked me down with a feather." This was Allison in full swing again; I moaned inside.

Hot-headed Allison, who didn't talk about it, didn't give anybody any choices, steams ahead towards a lot of trouble again. Not a lot I could do but accept her decision, I thought apprehensively. This is really showing the kind of mother she is, an impulsive, neglectful kind of parent. I wasn't very happy about it, but I managed to keep it to myself for the moment. I asked if she could she give me an idea when Jo would be back to the therapy room so that I could fix an appointment for him. The Social Services were referring many kids during that period, and I wouldn't want Jo to miss out on anything, especially now that the therapy was going well. He also would be able to plan ahead. No, she couldn't, but she would let me know soon, with a telephone call or a text message.

"Well, I see," I told her. "It looks like you have planned everything. I would have liked to have known much in advance, but there we are."

She continued to say that she was very sorry, but after what they had all gone through, it seemed to her the right thing to do. I just reflected on how many things in the past had looked like the right thing to do, according to her, and all of them had resulted in major disasters. I kept my mouth shut and, standing up from my position behind the desk, I accompanied the woman to the door and said: "Let's hope it is the right choice. I will wait for your telephone call and plan accordingly. Have a nice holiday and my regards to Jo and the rest of the family."

Allison was surprised by my sudden coldness, and left quickly saying "goodbye doc and thank you!"

She was having her way again, I thought, without taking anyone else into consideration; Her children, her pride in being a mother. For a moment, closing the door, I saw her hesitating as if she wanted to come back and then she stopped by the reception, and I saw her leaving an envelope to the secretary. I thought that would be a card from Jo saying goodbye.

I wasn't wrong. As I opened the envelope, I could recognize an abstract drawing with a big dotted thank you at the end and a few big numbers. They were the two missing digits on the combination lock, and they were different from my new ones. There was only one way to find out if he's right, I thought. I rushed to the toy box and found the lock.

I was Jo's age again!

Quickly I inserted the numbers, and then pushed the metal arm down a few times. Promptly the lock sprang open, and I shouted:

"Hurray. Well done Jo!"

Suddenly, it was summer and, after two more weeks, it was time for me to plan my holiday too. I couldn't think of anywhere I wanted to go. Lack of imagination on my side, or as usual memories from my childhood forbade me to do just that. My partner will have to decide, I thought with relief. Thank God for that because I am not the type who enjoys holidays so much. If it were up to me, I'd stay at home for two weeks. The city in high summer is quiet and pleasant. I could visit museums and galleries, which I didn't have time to do before because of my demanding job, and it would be a good opportunity to update all the records of my patients, which were still in the locked cabinet, rather than stored in the computer database.

I sat in my armchair by the window, for a change, looking at Jo's card and the numbers he had written down. I'll soon forget them; other kids will try to find them. I could hear his voice saying:

"This is about me, you and the playroom. Me inside, from the beginning to now!"

CHAPTER 10

THE ROUND TRIP HOME

Our minuscule post office and our lovely oversized postmistress epitomize our small-town country's well-being.

We are a happy bunch of people, although we have our life's problems, who doesn't? But we are the leg of Britannia, we Devonshire and Cornish folk.

I am sorry for you "townies," but I for one relish our plump hedgerows, milk churns, brown cows and so many country walks, creamy topped ale, and ruddy-faced friends.

Some of my mates are already married and breeders. I'll get married one day. I have a sweet girl in mind, Sarah is her name, she's fresh-eyed and gallant. Right now I am happy to kiss her and hug her, we have time. I am a "new one" on the boat, thanks to my brother and next "new one out," I hope.

I am thinking all these things as I wait with my Mum, Pa, and my sisters, for my brother to emerge from our old, little, Norman Church. With his bride and laughing faces, then off we all go to the wedding tea and proverbial wedding jokes and happiness, sure of our family unity.

Here they all come, the red-faced corpulent Vicar, bride, and groom, enthusiastically pursued by our village photographer, with our little cousin's bridesmaids picking their noses and adjusting their dresses. We are all safe in our hope that this will succeed, as sure as generations succeed and wither, succeed and wither, into infinity.

"You are next Jack," someone said to me amidst howls of friendly banter.

"Not me," I shouted in warm response. "I am the one that got away!"

Very soon the honeymooners mooned in their private place when the sun went down. We all wobbled our way back to our respective homes, thankful all had gone well.

"She's a nice girl. I think they'll make a good life," were my Pa's last words before negotiating the stairs to bed, after perhaps a jar too many.

Force ten gales and more have been known to whip up their revenge and thrash our coast into insensibility, many times before, not least this night as we lay bedded and safe.

I am thinking of my brother and bride, who by now would have cleared that temperamental metamorphic channel entangled in newness, enjoying their first week of the love tour they have so long prepared for.

"Has he asked to marry you?" he asked Sarah.

"Not yet dad, we are not in a hurry to wed."

"What is he waiting for? His brother is two years younger, and he got wedded last week."

His wife interrupted him; she knew where this conversation was going to lead.

"George, we were all there, remember?"

He ignored her and continued. "I wish I could say what I think of this house."

"I hear you, dad," the daughter answered gently. She loved her dad, and, on reflection, he made a lot of sense.

"You know Jack; he wants to buy a house before we get married."

"That's very well, but by the time he will be able to afford a house, you'll be 98 years old."

His wife laughed nervously but didn't say a thing.

"There's a little cottage by the sea, going for very cheap rent. What's wrong with renting? We've all been there; you could be settling there, start a family."

"Does he know that?" his wife interacted.

"Of course, he knows. His mate's father, Billy, is renting it!"

"Perhaps you should mention it to Jack when he comes back," the mother said.

"I will try, I promise," Sarah answered with a sigh.

"Did you hear what he said the day of his brother's wedding?"

"He was joking dad; you know that!"

"Nevertheless, it was a very strange thing to say in front of everybody. People talk, and we don't want to become the laughing stocks of the village, do we?"

"Of course not dad," she answered hoping the conversation would end.

The mother came to the rescue by saying: "Do you hear the storm? Never heard or seen anything like this. The waves are reaching the top of the cliffs. We are in for a good one! Come on old man, let's go to bed. Let's hope tomorrow will be a better day."

She put aside her knitting, and together they started to walk upstairs, saying "Goodnight darling, see you in the morning."

Sarah walked to the window and looked outside. The wind relentlessly bashed the coast. The storm was gathering more strength.

She couldn't help saying to herself, "Come back soon Jack. I don't care if you are marrying me or not. Come back home safe darling!"

The sharp interchange of tides and winds often whipped their unwanted revenge on this demure corner of little old England.

The revenge of the sea was for us, for taking so much and giving back little. They lashed our coast of Devon and Cornwall unremittingly, as the swells merged from the Irish Channel, which swallowed up the calmness of the Bristol waters.

The Channel fought bitterly against the onslaught of the not so far Atlantic, culminating in one almighty battle tearing at the coast and coves, breaking over the rocks for the entire world like Armageddon.

The volley of waves grabbed Nelly, as she gallantly slid slope in yet another brave effort to save yet another scream of despair, from the mighty, merciless jaws of the high sea.

From the Midnight Knock to the jetty in front of the oil tanker, Jack realized, apart from a few practice bouts that this was the big one, a giant oil tanker in need of help. His brother, who that week got married, would have responded to the call.

In terrified excitement, he leaped to his duty with his courageous friends against all the odds. The belly of the sea lifted the ship and threw it like a cork on Niagara.

Young Jack hung the rails and stared up in disbelief at the vast heaving and frothing of this huge laughing giant, as he continuously let them through, then smacked their bows to insensibility, leaving them deranged like babies taking a blow from a wild maniac.

All hell was assembled here, as the lifeboat pursued her course against inhuman odds.

The skipper cried: "ropes," as they neared the split victim. The tanker rolled and squirmed, then gave up her bows to the deep waters as they cracked, so easily, under this roaring monster.

Nelly moved forward, like a spitting kitten against a rabid Alsatian, and threw her lines for the remaining frantic crew, but to no avail; they were sucked by the vacuum into the bowels of this intrepid Goliath, never to be seen again.

The stern of the tanker rose in one last-ditch bellowing effort, before being grabbed by the depth, to shout no more.

The smell of oil, as she pumped out her gut, was now predominant. Jack heard the death rattle and saw no more.

"Nothing for us here," He heard the Skipper shout, "hold tight for the round-trip home."

His thoughts were running amok now, between white lace, and the little church, his pints, his mates, life, youth and the first sensation of love.

Nelly was lifted and squeezed like a lemon. The very deck on which Jack stood before his heroic gesture opened like an earthquake as he stood there. "I want to go home," he cried out, but there was no call for help, while his mates were swallowed alive with little or no struggle.

His girl and wedding bells, a house and children were Jack's ambition as he turned to concede. His strong fingers gripped the rails as he stretched his torso and blinked away the tears to face his foe.

His assailant took him gently, as he went into a dream.

The fathoms were quiet, and the storm was no more.

CHAPTER 11

All Systems Go

Samantha Rice stood at the graveside and peered into the dugout of six feet, as the bearers lowered the casket containing her mother taken after a long time suffering.

"Peace for you, at last, my dear Mom." My father, Jack, Sister Debbie, Roy, Tom, and grandchildren Vicky and Tim were there at Fern Head Cemetery.

"No flowers by request, all donations to the Royal Marsden, London SW3." This was the notice in the Evening Chronicle that day.

Roy, her husband, gripped her tightly as she peered through opaque eyes and burning tears at the coffin. It rocked shakily to a halt, and then sat where it would stay until all the living creatures on the hearth alive today, from the very last newborn baby, would be dead. All those new people alive after that might possibly dig it all up and turn it into an underground dwelling sight or a residential area. "Who knows?"

These and many other thoughts were crashing through Sam's confused and hurt mind on this sad occasion.

Her two brothers and sister with their respective spouses, Jack, her dad, and the rest of the gathered followers parted company early that evening and went back to their homes and sadness.

Jack was going to stay with Sam's sister for a while. It would take time, but he would recover from his staring disbelief and learn to live another day.

She had never really understood her mother, her mother had never really understood her, and there was nothing either of them could do about that.

The long, vile death with the disease of the century had taken its toll; it had what it wanted, and in its wake had left a trench of misery and uncertainty and a deluge of fear, which naturally scarred Sam, in her first close family tragedy. Now it was over, and for the first time in her life she understood real injury and indeed real life.

Roy

It was July now, six months after the January burial of her mother. Things were virtually back to normal, save her deep down underlying depression, which for some reason unknown to her Sam had never quite been able to dispose of.

She was forty years old, an attractive sociologist, married to Roy and the kitchen sink. She didn't mind so much being married to Roy, after all, she gave up her career to do just that, and have kids, so she knew what she was doing.

So did Roy, and all went well for a few years, and they were relatively happy when Roy began to work late at the office.

The verbal platitudes came to head one evening, in the late summer, when Sam felt depressed and sad.

"I'm not going on with this Roy,'" Sam said after one hell of a violent row.

"I am empty, and I am starving. I mean nothing, and I am doing nothing. We haven't even managed to have a child,' she moaned through trembling but determined lips.

She knew now, though, what she was never able to pinpoint when dealing with similar situations in her job, as a social worker.

She had to deal with cases of couples without education and emotionally less stable. She could never find a solution because she had never realized the feeling of a state of un-love. So, she did now!

Now she knew the hopelessness of the problem. She realized, like the sting of death, the heart is a slower healer than the flesh.

"I love you, Sammy Baby," Roy always used to call her that, when they first met in the throes of youthful passion. He was, and still is, a smasher, she thought. He's the same age; they grew to forty together and somewhere along the line these two attractive people lost their foothold and forgot to hold on to each other.

He also, as a social worker, had become more social than a worker, and in the affluence of status began to wallow in his prowess.

Chores of a domestic nature were never top of the list for Sam, but she tried to endure them dutifully. She spent years at work, advising families and children that taking drugs and mugging were wrong.

She did long for the arms of a person again, the need to touch and be loved. She was a striking lanky brunette with a desirable offbeat approach; her long legs, and steady stride turned many a head, and she knew it.

"I love you Sammy baby, I just can't figure out why we arrived at this," Roy sensitively told her.

"I'll tell you why, Roy, because you are messing around and you have forgotten how to love, and I don't need that! You are not going to heave me into middle age, no children, then go off and play musical chairs. Oh no, no! Get it right Roy and be quick about it."

Roy slammed the door and left the house; he had a call to make.

THE BANK

The teller, at the first window in the bank, glanced up as Sam walked in, then lowered his head and carried on ticking off the paying in a slip of his customer. She stood in the queue and glanced at the faces of the people in the queue, as they slowly shuffled their way to the appropriate light flash of a free window.

She morbidly began thinking, as she viewed some of the empty faces of the customers, of her mother's rotting corpse, and her own life's situation. Was she doomed to oblivion, or was there more? She could leave Roy now; she knew that!

The tightness in her stomach and vengeful jealousy had gone, she felt whole again.

Her blood was surging through her veins, she felt vibrant and alive, and that's the way she intended to stay.

"Miss... Miss, it's your turn," she heard a voice from window number one.

It wasn't her turn at all, but the woman before her was entangled in a busy conversation with another woman on the other side of the queue. The young guy, who posed a cursory glance as she entered the bank, had deemed it was.

"I am sure I've jumped the queue," she wistfully smiled.

"I know. Aren't you wicked?" he replied, holding her stare. His deep brown eyes, roofed by two immaculately laid dark brows, sat well balanced to the clean sweep and parted short hair. Sam had a clear view of his small, well-placed ears on that handsome, brusque, young face.

His eyes held her look. Finally, Sam pulled away and serenely opened her shoulder bag to get her checkbook, with slightly unsteady hands.

"Fifty pounds cash, please," she murmured quietly. "If I get lynched you'll be to blame," she threw in. "I'll come to your rescue," he mused.

"Haven't seen you before, Mrs. Rice," he continued looking at the name in the checkbook.

"That's because I don't like to spend too much money," she replied catching his cheeky but solemn stare at her again.

"Why not? That's what it's for," he said, stamping the check and counting out the cash.

"Tens, all right?" he asked.

"As it comes" she replied, clawing the money up in a nervous grab, and quickly making her escape.

She fled around the corner of the bank flushed with a feeling inside which she had quite forgotten.

"Mrs. Rice," yelled a voice behind her in the High Street, "Mrs. Rice, your checkbook, you forgot to pick it up."

The teller was facing her. She held out her hand to take the book from this creature, which would have looked better playing football than sitting in a bank. For the first time in quite a few years, Sam was stinging from the events of the day. "How ridiculous," she thought as she allowed her thoughts to play her tricks. "How ridiculous!" She smiled to herself as she fell into a very happy sleep that night.

Kevin was twenty-five, unmarried athletic and well sought after, and Sam summed him up in one go: "forbidden fruit."

A chance meeting at West Dibley railway station and two more cash withdrawals gave Kevin enough courage to approach Sam for a date.

She declined. A cash deposit and a fracas in the bank, namely interruption from some upset customers who said: 'you jumped the queue, young lady,' followed by the usual sheep-like murmurs of a typically English bank turnout, culminating in obscenities. Disgraceful, not right, ought to be stopped, etc. accelerated Sam's conceding to a meeting, and they did.

Kevin was besotted, Sam needed time.

"Mr. Grant, in future, will you be hyper-careful with queue control? We don't want a repeat of last week's nonsense."

That was the boring advice for Kevin from the area manager, as he was leaving the bank one evening to go to another one to bore them to death, with more inane advice.

"I am glad I caused a fiasco." He was saying to Sam during one of their stolen moments, "I made that sheep bleat their head off."

He was young and happy. A modern chap with a zest for living and an innate desire to love.

THE ESCAPE

Sam found herself on a BA flight to Rome, clutching the hand of an almost unknown person; "why and for what," he didn't know, but as it was, she was there with Kevin sat beside her, his warm hand wouldn't lose its grip.

She felt very relaxed and tremendously excited for the first time in a long period.

She began to reflect on all the events from the moment she said yes to a date with this young chap from the bank. She thought: "was I so miserable to leap at the first opportunity of affection? I couldn't possibly be so stupid, but I did, and I like him. He went to such a lot of trouble to please me, to make me feel like a woman again."

He looked happy and confident; she felt glad to be with him, a young man who cared. She concluded that both needed each other.

The hand squeezed tighter as he turned to look at her, his eyes were glazed and shining, he leaned over and kissed her: "Oh Sam, thank you for coming with me, I'll make you very happy, I promise."

On their first meeting, they had driven for miles, glancing, looking, touching and laughing about the situation at the bank and other stories. They told each other about their lives and aspirations.

They ate supper quietly and in an ambiance of serenity, at a small Inn on the outskirts of the New Forest and they both knew well enough when the evening was over that they felt attracted to each other and there was nothing they could do about it. They were a match, and **electrics were all systems go!**

An early morning phone call from Kevin had Sam leaping out of bed like a kangaroo. Roy was still asleep; it was Friday.

"Sam is that you?"

"Yes."

"Sam, we are both going to Rome this evening, that is, will you come with me?"

"What?" Sam answered shocked.

"Sam, make any excuse you can, we need each other, just come, don't ask how long, just do it!"

"Kevin, what are you saying? I can't leave just like that."

"Why not? I know you are hitched and I know you want to be with me, let's grab it, Sam, why not?" he insisted excitedly, "Let's just grab it and run!"

She began to panic, didn't want to ask any questions. This time she was caught at the right moment. Roy was indifferent and uncaring. Sam said yes and left a note for Roy.

Roy read the letter when he arrived home that Friday evening. He felt as if he had fallen like a piece of cement from a church steeple.

"Dear Roy, I have gone for a while. Don't send out the tracker dogs, just leave it be. I am perfectly safe; I am fed up with being taken for granted by you and everybody else. I have no further explanation. I need some space, and I am trying to sort out the situation between us. I'll be back soon with an answer or a solution, I hope. There's no other explanation. I just stopped breathing, and I need to come up for air."

KEVIN

Roy understood and left it at that. After all, he was in no position to blame her.

The plane touched down at Leonardo da Vinci Airport in Fiumicino, Rome. Kevin summoned a taxi at the lounge door and directed it to the Excelsior Hotel.

"Don't worry about the expenses Sam," he said. "My family is loaded, and I have an extended leave."

She asked no more questions. It wasn't important, she was quite independent anyway with a bundle of traveler's checks and a credit card: "I am going to show you the most beautiful country in the world," he uttered.

Kevin left their luxury suite to order drinks at the bar, while Sam put the final touches to her hair, after which they were to stroll in the evening air of Rome.

She emerged from the lift looking stunning in search of Kevin.

"Damn me, if it isn't Mrs. Rice," a strong voice interrupted her search. She looked surprised at the man in front of her smiling genuinely. She felt as if she wanted to hide amongst the people near her. "Who knows me? What does he want? How will he judge me?"

Finally, she stood right in front of him thinking: "I am not doing anything wrong, he can think what he likes, nothing to do with me!"

"Mr. Smith. Yes, it's me." She looked at the man now, and she remembered. He was her ex-boss when she worked for the Social Services in London. The head of the County Services to be precise, a big man with a big job. He always gave her a bad time, whatever she proposed to improve the services, particularly with young people. She used to call him "The old crow" because he opposed all modern innovations.

She never realized he was a very handsome man, tall and elegant. The years improved him, she thought.

"Are you here for the conference? I thought you had given up working?" he said with a genuine handshake.

"No, I am not. I'm here as a tourist."

"With a group?" He continued.

"Yes, sort of, a really small one." His eyes glinted away cheekily.

"You know, I was thinking about you last week, revising all the past improvement projects, and yours came up the best. Very relevant now and applicable, 15 years later."

"Well, maybe if you let me did my job then, some tragedy we heard on the news could have been avoided." She couldn't help herself saying. "Get on with them now; I won't charge you for them."

"You see, Mrs. Rice, they were other times, other politics and governments. I am pleased to see you haven't lost your fire."

"That will never go. Are you offering me the old job back?" she inquired in a joking tone.

"Well, I am offering an interview, yes. Just give me a call; you know where to find me. I am sure you could implement your projects now."

"I'll think about it. Now, if you will excuse me there is somebody waiting for me at the bar."

They parted from each other in a friendly manner.

Sam was looking at Kevin waiting there not far from where she was. They smiled at each other and together walked to the bar.

Sam couldn't stop looking at him and thought how many things had changed since they spent their first night in a hotel near the bank when Kevin finished his shift. That was about four weeks ago. She felt her metabolism had changed.

She had spent 15 long years looking at her pregnancy tests and every time they were negative, feeling like a failure. Now she felt she didn't need one, but she knew she was pregnant with Kevin's child and that filled her with joy and confidence. "No need to tell him yet," she thought, "not until the holiday is over and everything is settled nicely."

She had a devastating few years with Roy's infidelity, her uncertainty as a person, the death of her mother recently, which reduced her almost to believing she was a sludge, and nothing more than a sterile chambermaid.

In one fell swoop, she felt alive again. She felt as she had when she was twenty. This one crazy mission into ecstasy had refilled the confidence barometer.

She'd found what she thought she had lost forever. Her clear angular face was heavenly and wanton.

Kevin led her wanton; their nights were whiled away, inhuman fusion and days of searching, traveling and finding.

They hung a silver thread on every star they discovered in the galaxies and Kevin was elated and fulfilled.

She traveled the unknown green pastures with her lover. He was much younger, she knew it, but who cared?

Together they cracked the uncertainty, waded through the quicksand to find the crystal-clear stream of perfect harmony and they drank their fill, and then lay back exhausted.

They flew to Venice and traveled on the Orient Express. They climbed Mount Etna and swam in the bay of Napoli. They visited Pompeii, Herculaneum and the fortresses of Porto Ecole.

Never for a moment were these two-lost lovers disentangled.

The innocence of their adulthood and lavish togetherness could not bring their fairytale to an end until one day, on the twenty-second of September, the money ran out, and the party was over.

THE RETURN

The plane landed at Heathrow, on a cold chilly dark late September evening and the two emerged silently and tangled. Their silence was extended throughout the short haul to the passenger bay and customs area.

They were looking at each other through glued eyes and his hands held her tightly, as they passed through the arrival gate and into the main hall.

Sam spotted Roy in the queue of people waiting for their friends and family.

"How did he know I was coming back?" she couldn't help thinking.

A sharp voice and some flashing lights interrupted her train of thought.

"Mr. Kevin Grant?"

"Yes," he answered confidently.

"I am Detective Superintendent Smith. I am arresting you for questioning about the twenty-five-thousand-pound deficit at the bank..."

Those words, and all that was happening felt like a nightmare to Sam, who was about to faint.

Her legs went numb, and she wanted to disappear from the scene.

"Was all that true? How could he have put me in such a situation? My family, my friends, all the world will know about it!"

She felt Roy's hand pulling her outside the circle of police, photographers and curious people wanting to know what was happening.

She looks a last glance at Kevin, who turned to her and smiled.

"You see Sam? I believed I could never have you. Believe me; I would crack open the vaults of the Bank of England for you and shower you with gold petals. I love you!"

He managed to scream out, while the two policemen were pulling him, handcuffed towards the exit.

"Come along sir," were the last words Sam heard as she felt Roy still holding her and pulling her further away.

"Shut up you lunatic," she heard him saying angrily.

"Let go of me, now! You are hurting me! She screamed at Roy. "I don't need you, go away!"

Her final stage of the journey back to the city was an emotional travesty, and she stepped from the last bus into the lights, along with drunks of the night and screaming party girls.

She slowly walked along in the streets. She needed time to reflect on the whole happening.

She walked for hours, thinking about the best moments of their adventures and the love and tenderness which Kevin gave her, without reserve and conditions. She couldn't help thinking:

"If a man would rob a bank for me, he's worth waiting for," and she cried and cried.

CHAPTER 12

Island, A family

If you think you are going to pick cedars once you arrive, you will be disappointed. The island takes its name from a load of the fruit that ended up on its beaches from a shipwreck.

The village people are very nice, and they mind their own business.

The nice thing about the island is that the climate is warm, and the sea is never far away from where you are.

The inhabitants are very proud, hard-working people, quite reserved. Mario used to say ironically that it was easier to land on the moon than to be accepted as a friend on the island!

Very different from where he came from, the mainland, "the Continent," as they called it.

There, they are friendlier, more open and inclusive. There have been, of course, episodes with which he didn't agree, in both places, but is there a perfect place to live? You tell me if you know of one!

Another thing they do there is given nicknames to everyone. Some of them are horrible, and once you get yours, you stick with it for the rest of your life. It's like an unwanted family coat of arms.

Personally, he didn't approve of that custom; it's demeaning and degrading to the person who is landed with one of them. Sometimes, it's the description of private parts, and you wonder how they got to know it. He passionately hoped that one day that habit would cease for good.

On the other hand, they are very generous people and go out of their way to help you. He often thinks of them with affection, friendliness, and nostalgia.

Very different from the island, as Mario soon found out, where everything has a price.

The villagers are mainly fishermen or sailors. The tourists, those who own houses or villas in the area, who come from other parts of the island, mainly professionals, are considered 'not like us,' and they are treated with studied kindness and indifference. People from the "continent" are often described with compassion because 'they don't clean their house like us' or 'they are always on the phone' and so on.

In all, Mario liked them, because at least he knew where he stood with them, and, they are very genuine, nice people.

ISLAND 1979

The Ferryboat's siren echoed in the distance. Mario is in the kitchen of his restaurant on the island seafront, cutting vegetables on the metal table.

"What am I thinking about now?" He asked himself. "That's the past; I am here now. My children were born here; my business is here, never mind the past."

"Signor Ma, good morning. I brought you some fish. It's beautiful and fresh... do you want it?"

A familiar voice, Nani the fisherman, coming for some money.

Mario stopped chopping nervously; then he looked at the fish without enthusiasm.

"What is it?"

"Calamari and mullets and some plaice."

"No thank you. I have got six kilos from last week."

"Eh, that's ready for the rubbish bin, I'll give you some discount, ok?"

Nani put the fish on the kitchen scale; he is a young man twenty-five years old. Mario saw him grow from a little tot into an athletic, handsome lad. "Are you listening?" I said. "No thank you!"

"Not even eight thousand per kilo... I have been all day in the water."

"Aren't you working for the ferry as well?"

"So what, Signor Ma?"

"Well," Mario continued, "You are off duty at seven; it's eleven now so... you have been fishing for four hours."

Nani smiles and says: "Hey, you are well informed, Signor Ma, I was only joking."

"I was joking as well. That's your business. The truth of the matter is that business is bad now. The tourists are rare; the season had a bad start, it rained all through April."

Suddenly he interrupts him. "Signor Cartas is working well. Toretto sold him thirty kilos of fish in a week."

"You know the story," Mario responds on the patronizing side. "He's got regulars, and he was born here; everybody sends clients to him from the ferry boat."

"Come on Signor Ma; you are unjust now, if he works more than you do, there must be a reason."

"Yes, two young German girls serving in miniskirts."

Nani is getting interested now: "Why don't you do the same thing? You are still young, divorced, and free."

"I see, you are well informed,"

Nani continued: "When your daughter was here, things were different."

"I know, she was even speaking your language."

"She was sympathetic; she knew how to treat the customers."

"Yes, she gave them everything."

Nani gets impatient now with Mario's innuendo. "Signor Ma, you are talking about your daughter."

He's now throwing a handful of salt in the soup pot.

"And you were dipping your fingers in it. Come on, no need to get offended, I would have liked you as a son-in-law, but I am a man who looks at reality, you should know me by now."

"Yes, I know you, but sometimes you are a bit too hard, especially where the family is concerned."

Toni, Mario's Kitchen assistant, a young boy of 19, comes in and interrupts the conversation.

"That's true; I often tell him that."

He's stirring the soup now, "who's asking you, Miss Goody-Two-Shoes?"

"Sorry. I know her well; she's my best friend, nobody could understand her around here."

"She was a good ally, wasn't she?"

Nani is now getting ready to go: "I think she had more than one. Signor Ma, I add it to the bill, see you later."

"Right, in the end, they always do what they want with me! He keeps muttering while tasting the soup."

"Puah, too much salt." He looks at Toni who is peeling the potatoes by the sink.

"How many times have I told you to mind your own business?" Toni is ignoring him now.

"Everybody is always ready to judge other people's actions. When my wife left me for that German dandy, you people found something to say, as if it was my fault, mine!"

The boy is now getting upset; he stops peeling the potatoes: 'What's all that got to do with your wife? That happened ten years ago. We are talking about Marianna, your daughter.'

"Have I sent her away? What does a man have to do to keep his own integrity, his own respect?"

Toni is baffled now by his statement. "I don't understand you!"

"Yes, of course, you don't understand me, who does? Anyway, it's too late; nobody wants to understand an older man, if anything he's got to try to understand the young generation if he can manage to keep out of the slaughterhouse for a few more years..." Toni, after a moment of hesitation, interrupts him.

"Talking about the slaughterhouse Signor Ma, did you buy some meat? The last steak left us last night."

"Oh... Jesus Christ, I forgot!"

Gavi, Mario's son, is 21. A tall, striking, young man wearing torn jeans and a ring through his nose and his lower lip.

"Morning Pa!"

"Here is the son of my youth, the firstborn, the flesh of my flesh, bones of my bones..."

"Alright dad, you made your point, save me from that!" He looks at Toni with a grin on his face then he continues:

"Two fussy Milanesi are at the bar, they'd like to book a table. They want to know," he says imitating the voice of a fussy customer from Milan, 'Is it fresh or is it frozen?' 'Could we see it?'"

Mario is now throwing a kitchen cloth on the table:

"I bet you told them frozen!" He moans getting out of the kitchen. "Now he tells me, 20 minutes later."

They are both laughing at Mario's expense.

"He always falls for that! What's the matter with the grumpy old man? I haven't seen him so upset for donkeys' years."

"I don't know; we were talking about your sister."

"Oh, that one! You are playing the wrong symphony."

"It wasn't me. It was Nani."

"Who else? For Nani, only two things exist, beer and Marianna."

"He talks well about her."

"I bet. He went bananas about her. Can you imagine? Marianna with a fisherman!"

"I have seen worse things."

"Me too!" Toni is getting annoyed and interrupts Gavi by saying:

"Come on; you know what I am talking about. She's coming back soon. I got a letter from her last week. I wanted to tell your father, but I couldn't find the courage. Are you going to tell him about Marianna?"

"Listen, I mind my own business. I am already in trouble with the old man. It's a question of survival. Give him a surprise. His life is becoming so tedious in this blob of land lost in the sea. Ok? Let's give him a surprise."

Mario comes back to the kitchen a few minutes later.

"They've gone, your pedantic Milanesi."

"Never mind Pa, we'll get some more. And some Torinesi too." Mario looks disinterested now, but he carries on moaning.

"A good idea, Pa, listen: let's do it like in that restaurant in Porto Verde; the client raises his finger, points to the lobster and a moment later it's on the grill... alive."

"And who's going to catch the lobster, you?"

Toni joins in the conversation, "they are so expensive these days."

"I am not a fisherman," says Gavi annoyed by his father's innuendos.

"I know. You are not a restaurateur either, or a builder. You are not...."

"Go on...same old story. If you don't know who to blame, blame the unemployed."

"Unemployed? You could still be in the Army; they wanted you. You were good with the rifles."

"I didn't want them," shouts Gavi getting angry now.

"You could have stayed two more years. Your barber in the meantime would have learned how to cut hair."

"It's useless trying to discuss anything with you when you are in this mood."

"I am not in a mood. Mine are real observations. Am I not allowed to express myself in human fashion, mouth, throat, and voice?" Now Mario is mocking his son's voice. "I beg your pardon, ladies, and gentlemen if I don't get my microphone or the latest ultrasonic gadget. I'll try to do my best."

Toni, is trying to get out of the discussion by saying: "Signor Ma, can I go out for a moment?"

"You as well... we must try and work now. We have been in a siesta the whole winter."

"Was that directed at me?" Gavi asked his father.

"Oh no, I wouldn't dare," he responded to him, while Toni is now pressing for attention.

"Please, can I go? It's urgent.'

"Go, go, if you must. You spend days on the telephone."

Gavi now finds an opportunity to get back at his father. "You know your trouble, don't you?"

"No, I don't. Tell me; I'm all ears."

"You want to control the lives of everybody who has the misfortune of being near you."

There is sadness now in Mario's voice as he responds to his son. "Yes, and usually it's too late. Sometimes I ask myself, is it worth raising a family, to look after your children?"

"To feed them, clothe them, help them when they are in need," Gavi continues while his father is ignoring him.

"On the other hand, I can't even complain. You and your sister have got your diploma... after much aggravation. It's not your fault if you can't find a job. I am a poor old stupid man, thinking that you two would have taken up this business," he continued. "Got to be joking! Among the kitchen smells? One wants to dress up in the latest fashion. The trend is wasted in a restaurant, it's boring, always there looking after the till, the bar, the people, or in the smelly kitchen."

Gavi is now putting his arm on Mario's shoulder: "Pa, you mustn't take it like that!"

"I know, son. It's about your mother. Sometimes I am tortured with nightmares."

He's surprised by his father's answer.

"That happened a long time ago dad. You mustn't think about it."

"Easier said than done, I can assure you of that.'" His voice is sad; he looks on the verge of crying.

"Don't get me wrong, son, I don't give a damn about your mother now. I am talking about the reasons, the truth. I still can't find an answer." Now he looks at Gavi with compassion and goes further saying: "Poor you, both of you! It must've been a terrible shock, to lose her suddenly, like that."

"I told you, it's not worth thinking about it. We understood."

"Did you son, why didn't you explain it to me?"

"We understood the situation, Dad, we understood you. In other words, we didn't blame you for that. Most of the time she was under the influence of alcohol, and then, when she met him, we suspected other things too, especially Marianna."

"Marianna, how did she take it, son? Not long after, she left us too."

"The same, Dad, believe me."

"She was so attached to her mother. I always believed she was behaving in that awkward manner to make me pay for it, to revenge her mother."

"Revenge? What are you talking about? Also, Marianna loves you."

"If she loves me," Mario continues, "why has she gone?"

"Teenager crisis, she felt she had to go to explore the big world over the sea. Just like I did."

"But at least I knew where you were, in the army." He pauses now his voice is tired, but he's still exploring.

"You could be right. I am old fashioned, but I am not stupid, you know!"

"I know pa, sure I know."

"You must try to understand my situation."

"I understand the situation!" Gavi said, getting tired now of the same conversation. "Look son. I don't consider myself finished. I have had a wrong marriage, and shortly I'll be reaching my fifties. If anything, it's an incentive to behave in a certain way."

"I am not following you, Dad."

"At least we are talking, son. It's like one's political idea; you have your idea in politics, don't you?"

"Sure, I got it, and I can't change it,"

"I am like your political idea, son. It can be wrong, but I can't change it!" At this moment,

Toni comes into the kitchen sobbing. Gavi looks at him relieved by the interruption:

"What happened now? Don't tell me your boyfriend has dropped you again. You two are like cat and dog. Now, come here."

Mario is trying to comfort him, "it's time to get ready for the rush!"

That usually takes him out of his teenager's passion. His sense of duty is stronger than his disappointment.

The kitchen gets alive again.

Signor Loreddo is a great contributor to the island, and so is his wife, Martinetta. They are both verging on the right wing of politics. They have both been sympathizers of Mussolini, in fact they are still talking about him with enthusiasm and nostalgia.

"That didn't happen when Mussolini was in charge, etc."

They were always forecasting a disaster and bankruptcy.

"You'll see what will happen shortly. It's like anarchy, look at them, cars, holidays, new houses! Where will all this take us?"

They were relatively well-off people. Mind, Signor Loreddo had been working all his life in the police force, but now he's retired. They were both from well to do families with properties and land in the country but didn't show off their status. They talked to anyone, hoping underneath to convert them to their way of thinking, without pressure and concerning their political views. They would offer help and advice, if they were asked for it, freely if it was possible for them to give it. They were always kind and generous. They have two sons, who often come to visit them.

Signora Martinetta must have been a very good-looking woman when she was young. She was always well dressed and well coiffured. They were always together. They both enjoyed a little gossip, but, like the rest of the village, it was never malicious or unfounded.

Mario is listening to him saying his wife had to go away for family reasons:

"I told her. Dear, if you really must go, then go! You might as well while you're there do something about your sciatica. Our clinics perform miracles, you know. She likes to go there; her sister lives nearby, she has a fine house with a beautiful garden, she lives with her mother, a woman well over ninety, full of energy. I remember in 1968, when I was there, she was digging the garden like a teenager. I have asked myself many times, where she gets all that energy from!"

Mario is getting tired now of listening to him.

"Also, my mother was like that! Now for dessert, what can I get you?"

He continued, ignoring Mario. "My wife, now, I always say to her, you'll live till you are a hundred. Listen! I have been told some stories about her mother. Sometimes children are cruel towards their parents, and when her time comes there will be a lot of discussion and controversy... I know, a woman who worked all her life. She buried two husbands, I know, not very lucky in that aspect, but they left her well..."

Mario is now looking at another table where two clients hadn't had their first course yet.

"They have ordered two spaghetti al ragu, Mario tells Toni who's in the kitchen."

"No Signor Ma, I remember very well. You ordered two fish risottos!"

"Wait!" Mario finally says. "I'll ask them again."

That's the life on an Island, in a restaurant! He's now sitting behind the bar, talking to a young couple on honeymoon.

The young man is speaking, looking tenderly at his wife and holding her hand.

"We didn't think it was so beautiful, so natural. Our sea is polluted. We did the right thing to come here on our honeymoon."

"When you are on honeymoon, everything is beautiful," Mario suggested.

"That is not true," she intercepted. "We went to Corfu for a few days, we were disappointed."

"Sure, there is no comparison! Our country is the most beautiful country in the world, shame about other things."

"Hey, that's enough! We don't want to talk about politics, not now anyway. Here I feel free, far from anywhere," reprimanded his wife.

I hope nothing will happen like last year in a similar situation, Mario thought; the bride fell in love with a local sailor and the groom went back to Torino on his own. The news was all over the island.

Finally, the honeymooners left for their hotel when Nani and Toretto came in probably on the last tour of the local bars.

"The ferry-boat was packed," said Nani, "they are coming in thousands."

"Where do they go? They are not stopping here!"

"The coast is full of tourists; they don't know where to put them!" He continued.

"Lucky for them! Here we are, waiting for the summer and when it finally arrives, they go off somewhere else."

Toretto, a young man, a friend of Nani, now joins in the conversation. "It's also true; you always complain Signor Ma!"

"Listen to him. A man who takes home two million lire per month, plus the fishing. It's not worth having a business anymore."

"Hey, Signor Ma, don't exaggerate! Two million per month?"

"Ah, you see ... when you get near the truth?"

"Let's talk about the Swedish girl you keep upstairs."

"Listen, I lived for ten years in Sweden from when I was eighteen, then I had all the Swedish girls I ever wanted."

"Why did you come back, then?"

"Because I am crazy, I was so happy there!"

"I bet you went there to avoid doing your National Service in the army!"

"It was one of the reasons."

"We blame the kids now; what about the fathers, then? I had to do two years in the navy. That was the real National Service. Not now! They go on holiday."

"Two more beers please," the other ordered abruptly. Obviously, he had heard the story before.

"It's midnight, time to go to bed you two!"

"Now you have been nasty."

"I get up early in the morning, you know?"

"For what? No clients..."

"Come on, you two… out."

"Ok, ok," moaned Nani finally, "Let's go, and don't keep the Swedish girl waiting."

"No danger of that. She's my son's girlfriend. I don't think he needs any help from you two."

They both left laughing at Mario.

The voice of Toni could be heard from the kitchen.

"Can I go Signor Ma?"

"Sure, I thought you'd gone!"

"I had to put the fish in the freezer. Don't forget to buy the meat. We've finished it."

Mario couldn't help saying: "I don't believe it! An Island, fish everywhere and everybody eats meat. They ask you: what kind of fish do you have? You give them the full list, and after that, they say: I'll have a steak, please!" He moaned imitating a fussy customer.

The restaurant is now closed. Mario is checking the accounts sitting upstairs in his studio.

He fell asleep in his chair. The deep sound of the siren on the ferry-boat just docking into the harbor woke him up. Five o' clock already, he thought.

It followed the rusty noise of the train, coming out of the ferry's mouth, and finally cars and foot passengers.

It was then when he heard continuous banging on the door.

Slowly and reluctantly, he opened the door to find a young woman outside holding a small suitcase. Her hair was black and untidy, almost covering her face. She was crying.

From her voice, a lot of memories came back from when his daughter was a child, and she used to whimper in that way.

"Marianna, is it you?"

She stopped crying for a moment. She tried to compose herself pulling her hair back with her fingers, and then she said: "Yes Dad, it's me, please help me. I have been raped."

"What do you mean? Who... did that? Where? Come in darling, what...?" Mario was now panicking. The news sent him into a kind of shock, which was making him feel helpless and numb as if somebody or something was sucking the strength out of him. "Who did this to you? Where?"

"Last night," she cried out. "I watched television at the bar for an hour or so; then I went downstairs to my cabin. My cabin was situated at the end of a long corridor. I was getting the key out of my purse when a door suddenly opened, and I was pushed into the cabin by a man." She paused now in distress. I screamed out, but, he covered my mouth with his hand, I couldn't breathe. Then he pointed a knife at my throat and said if I didn't shut up he would cut my throat."

Mario was holding Marianna tightly now, to comfort her. "I was terrified, I struggled, but he punched me hard in my face. He said he would throw me into the sea. I've done it before, he said, nobody will help you. It'll be just another body on the beach."

"Did you tell anyone on the ship?" Mario asked in a broken voice.

"No, Dad, I didn't. I don't want anyone to know this." He couldn't believe what he was hearing.

"Look at you! Look at what that criminal has done to you. We must go to the police now!"

"I will not go to the police. I don't want anybody to know this."

"How can you say that? He'll carry on doing this to other women. He said he killed somebody already."

"I am sorry. I don't want to tell anyone."

"But why? Why? They'll catch him if you do. Tell them about the cabin, the number... Was it next to yours?"

"They'll blame me for it; I know how it goes in this situation. I know the number, but I will not tell you."

"I still don't understand..."

"He said he knows me, knows where I live. He would come for me. I know he would."

"Maybe he was bluffing..."

"Dad... I don't want to take the chance, and I don't want to go through all the rape procedure."

"Things are different now; it will be a private and fast procedure, I'll make sure of that."

"No, it won't... promise me you will not tell anybody about this." She was waiting for his answer with determination. He did not answer.

"Dad, promise or I'll leave, right now!"

Mario knew she meant it. He knew her from when she was a child, honest, but stubborn like her mother. She would leave in that state, he thought.

There was nothing for him to do but to say:

"I promise. I promise."

They cried together, holding each other tightly.

Marianna, for the first time in a long time, felt safe and protected.

Mario's feeling didn't last long. Suddenly, he remembered the news three years ago.

The body of a young girl was found on the beach about fifty kilometers away.

It was on the local and national TV news every day for a long period because it was very difficult to find out her identity. The body had been in the water for a long time.

It also proved difficult to establish the motive for her death.

The police and forensic team thought she swam too far and was overpowered by the strong current.

After a careful search of all missing people nationally, with the dates of their disappearance, sex and situation, the team came out with dozens of identities.

Finally, it was possible to identify the girl.

The parents came to the island and, thanks to a tiny birthmark on her body, recognized their daughter, age 19, who had left home a month previously for an unknown motive.

After a long and complete investigation, this was confirmed.

The verdict was 'accidental death,' and the case was closed.

The parents were distraught, and they never believed this to be the case. She was a very confident swimmer and, knowing the daughter's character, it was most unlikely that she swam so far out to sea.

They tried to reopen the case, to no avail. They are still searching the island in pursuit of the reason for the daughter's death.

Marianna stirred and looked at her father. 'I feel you are distant now. What are you thinking about?'

She was still crying. He looked at her face; her eyes were red, and there was a big bruise on her face. She cleared her hair away, and he could see a red ring round her neck.

He felt a strong sense of rage towards the animal that did that to his daughter

"I am thinking about you darling, what you went through." He's holding her face, kissing her forehead tenderly, as he used to do when she was a little girl.

"Don't worry darling; it will be our secret." He told her in reassurance. But in his mind a weird voice was telling him: "I've done it before; nobody will help you. It'll be just another body on the beach."

He was smiling at himself now, thinking: "Don't worry Marianna, nobody will know what he's done to you, but I will not rest until he's caught and put away forever. I promise you that!"

There was silence everywhere now. The island was still asleep.

Mario was relieved now by the thought of vindication.

They both hugged, knowing that they had found each other again.